INFOGRAPHICS
A JOURNALIST'S GUIDE

INFOGRAPHICS
A JOURNALIST'S GUIDE

JAMES GLEN STOVALL
UNIVERSITY OF ALABAMA

Allyn and Bacon
Boston · London · Toronto · Sydney · Tokyo · Singapore

ISBN 0-205-26105-1

Printed in the United States of America

10 9 8 7 6 5 4 3 2 1   00 99 98 97 96

Table of contents

1   **BEYOND THE PARAGRAPH**   **1**
Beyond the words, 4
The graphics revolution, 4
Deadlines and the graphic journalist, 7
The development of infographics, 9
Developing an award-winning graphic, 13
Disadvantages of graphics, 14
Do graphics help the reader? 15

2   **PRINCIPLES OF GRAPHIC PRESENTATION**   **19**
Design principles, 20
Conventions of graphics, 26
The good graphic: tips from the pros, 30
Toward the good graphic, 31
Categorizing infographics, 33

3   **CHART-BASED GRAPHICS**   **35**
Representing numerical data, 36
Elements in a chart, 37
Bar charts, 41
Column charts, 47
Line charts, 50
The tyranny of the alphabet, 55
Pie charts, 56

4   **MAPS**   **61**
The modern map, 63
Locator maps, 65
Data maps, 68
Developing a map file, 69
Explanatory maps, 75
Getting creative, 77

5   **CHARTS WITHOUT NUMBERS**   **79**
Process charts, 80
Structure charts, 82
Time charts, 87
Building charts, 90

6   TYPE-BASED GRAPHICS   93

Development of type, 93
Anatomy of type, 98
Type on the page, 100
Using type, 102
Type as a graphic device, 106
Attention-getting type, 114

7   ILLUSTRATION-BASED GRAPHICS   117

Purposes of illustration-based graphics, 120
Creating illustrations, 127
Profile of a newspaper illustrator, 129
Copyright: swiping ideas without breaking the law, 131
Legal and ethical considerations, 132

8   ERRORS AND INACCURACY   137

Sources of error, 140
Common practices, 145
Avoiding error, 152

9   MAKING GRAPHICS WORK   153

A general approach to developing graphics, 154
Developing graphics, 155
But my newspaper is too small to have a graphics department, 156
Tips for the small newspaper that wants to get into graphics, 157
Procedures, 161
Principles, 162

GLOSSARY   163

INDEX   173

Preface

The poet William Wordsworth wrote these lines of lament in the first half of the 19th century:

> *Now prose and verse sunk into disrepute*
> *Must lacquey a dumb Art that best can suit*
> *The taste of this once-intellectual Land.*
> *A backward movement surely have we here,*
> *From manhood,–back to childhood . . .*
> *Avaunt this vile abuse of pictured page!*
> *Must be all-in-all, the tongue and ear*
> *Nothing? Heave keep us from a lower stage!*

William Wordsworth
from a print in
Harper's magazine, 1850

Wordsworth was decrying the growth of illustrated books and newspapers, something he envisioned as less intellectually stimulating than simply words on a page. Illustrations would lure people away from words, he feared, and turn them into children.

Wordsworth should neither have worried nor have been so narrow-minded. Men and women were using pictures to communicate long before they had words. The word is not the only form of communication worthy of our use; nor is it necessarily intellectually the "highest' form of communication. Leonard da Vinci demonstrated this when he wrote in his journals. The master intellect of his age wrote words as long as words were useful to him. When they were not useful, he drew pictures – right beside the words (see page 10). He did this in the days before graphic interfaces in computers. Today, we live in a privileged age – one in which our technology allows us to integrate words with pictures and other graphic forms. Thus, we should take full advantage of the opportunities that have been given to us to communicate our information and ideas.

This book is written in the spirit of Leonardo. That is, we should use whatever form of communication that presents our information and ideas in the best and most efficient manner to the reader. But doing that requires a knowledge of what those forms are and how they should be used. This book is designed to help us understand graphic forms and to use them properly in our communication activities.

Many people have contributed to this book in many different ways. I have leaned heavily on the work of Nigel Holmes, Edward Tufte, Howard Finberg, Bruce Itule, Tim Harrower, Sandra Utt, Steve Pasternak, John Noble Wilford, Anna Rogers, William C. Brinton, Edmund Arnold, the many contributors to *Design* magazine, and many others active in the Society of Newspaper Design who maintain high standards for graphic presentation and who generously share their work and ideas with others. In particular, I need to thank the following people:

Jack Smith, who wrote many of the sidebars for this book and had one good idea after another all the time;

Stacey Sweat, Ernest Hart, Scott Davis, Dan Procter, Gordon Preece, Bruce Diller, Joy Gehr and others who allowed me to use their work as examples in this book;

Ed Mullins, dean of the College of Communication at the University of Alabama, who was constantly encouraging to me in producing this work;

Members of my 1996 spring semester Advanced Editing class, including Staci Alexander, Scott Darling, Jud Lee, Wayne Phillips, Ben Pines, Carrie Weeks, Mark Cerny, Mike Jarosi and Delores Vinson, who gave me valuable help in the final stages of proofreading this book;

And finally, and most of all, to Sally and Jeff; they put with with all this and more and without them the book would not exist.

INFOGRAPHICS
A JOURNALIST'S GUIDE

Beyond the paragraph

When word reached the *Chicago Tribune* in January 1993 that seven people had been killed in a restaurant in Palatine, just north of Chicago, the newsroom sprang into action as it normally would on a big, breaking story. Reporters were pulled from other assignments to talk with relevant sources and provide background about the event. Photographers were sent to the scene to take what pictures they could. Editors began planning their presentation of what they could find out about this tragic event.

Another set of the *Tribune's* journalists – the graphics coordinators and artists – began working on the story at the same time. A decade before, they would have not been brought into the story until late in the day, and on many newspapers would not have existed at all.

On that January morning in Chicago, they participated in the *Tribune's* coverage from the very beginning. Stacy Sweat, the paper's recently hired art director, heard about the story from the overnight metro editor at about 9:45 a.m. She assigned Tracy Hermann, a graphics coordinator, and Laura Stanton, a graphics artist, to the story. They, in turn, began to plug themselves into the staff's efforts to find out what had happened and why.

Throughout the day journalists from the Tribune worked to fill out the story. Two graphics journalists on the scene made sketches of the building and interviewed employees to confirm their information and impressions. These sketches were faxed to the paper's art department where Dave Jahntz had been working on a map of the area. At the Page 1 meeting at 3:30 p.m., the editors considered using photographs as the major art, but because of the preliminary sketches that Stacy Sweat had made, they decided on using an informational graphic instead. The graphics journalists continued to work on the graphic right up to the first deadline at 8 p.m. It included a number of items that various people had been gathering throughout the day, including a cutaway of the building, three maps, a list of the victims, a chronology of events, and several other typographic items. Between 8 and 10:30 p.m., they edited and updated the graphic for the final edition.

Nearly six months later in Jackson, Mississippi, three workers were injured when they fell about 30 feet from a platform that was being lifted by a crane. All three were hospitalized, but none was seriously hurt. Still, it was a high profile accident. The men had been working on "The Stack," an interchange bridge where Interstates 55 and 20 and U.S. highway 49 meet near the Pearl River. The accident, which occured about 5:45 p.m., backed up rush hour traffic for an hour and a half.

The massacre at the Palatine restaurant near Chicago in 1993 presented the graphics staff of the Chicago Tribune with an opportunity to work in concert with other reporters and editors to produce some outstanding graphic presentations of information about that news event.

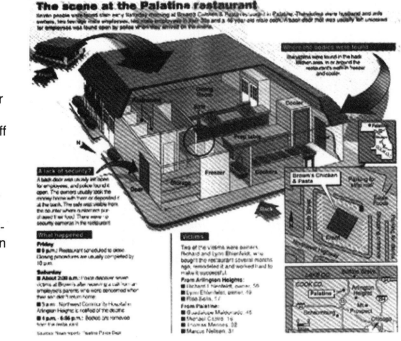

The newspaper clipping headline reads:

3 workers injured on I-55 'Stack'

Men tumble from platform lifted by crane

By Tori Lopaska
Clarion-Ledger Staff Writer

The Jackson (Miss.) Clarion-Ledger used a variety of forms to tell their readers about an accident at a construction site. One of the members of the graphics department was on the scene doing sketches along with the reporter and the photographer.

The *Clarion-Ledger* sent a photographer and reporter to the scene, but the editors also dispatched Godfrey Jones, one of the newspaper's four-person art staff. He checked out the scene and talked with witnesses. In about an hour he produced a graphic that dramatically demonstrated what had happened to the men.

What the *Chicago Tribune* and the *Clarion-Ledger* produced on these days was not only a full written account of the events and photographs that showed the scene after the fact, but also graphics that put the readers directly into the story. The graphics pictured for readers what the words and photographs could not do. They helped explain the what, where and why of the story in ways that traditional forms of conveying information could not.

BEYOND THE WORDS Many a journalist has loudly and proudly proclaimed, "I'm a *word* person." The meaning of that statement has never been clear, although it often reflects an individual's antipathy toward numbers or the supposed inability to handle them. While never a particularly intelligent or accurate description even of those who have made the statement, the declaration of being a "word person" is more irrelevant now than it has ever been for journalists. While words are still the most common means of communication for the journalist, they are in no way the only means, and on occasion they are not the most effective tools a journalist can use.

The picture, chart or graph has always been a powerful way to convey information to a reader or viewer. The fact that newspapers, magazines and other publications are using them more these days does not represent any discovery on the part of journalists. What it does reflect is the development of technology that allows these forms to be created and published more easily and a recognition by journalists that there are many means of presenting information. Journalists, just as their readers, live in a visual world where pictures, lines, charts, drawings and graphs are just as prevalent as words – and now, almost as easy to produce. In order to function well in this world of expanded information forms, the journalist of today must be able to understand and use a variety of means of expression. Self limitations, such as expressions that they are "word persons," do not enhance the credibility or the marketability of today's journalists.

Many publications have recognized the necessity of going beyond the paragraph. They have established staffs of graphic artists and journalists who actively participate in the coverage of the news and the presentation of information, just as we have seen in the story of the *Chicago Tribune's* coverage of the Palatine tragedy. The *Chicago Tribune* has a staff of 16 graphic artists and coordinators. The *Clarion-Ledger* in Jackson has four graphic artists plus a graphics editor on the news staff.

The trend toward more emphasis on graphics is not just a fad. Most publications now recognize that they need to present information in a variety of ways and that their readers are being trained to expect more visual presentations. In a 1989 study of 161 daily newspapers with circulations of more than 25,000, Sandra Utt and Steve Pasternack found most of the papers had been redesigned during the previous five years and that they were using more color and graphics. They concluded that ". . . graphics specialists in most newsrooms are changing attitudes as well as design."

THE GRAPHICS REVOLUTION There is little doubt among today's journalists that we have undergone a "graphics revolution." Readers are being presented – some would say "assaulted" – with more visual infor-

Graphic representations of information
come in a wide variety of forms thtat
we will explore in this book.

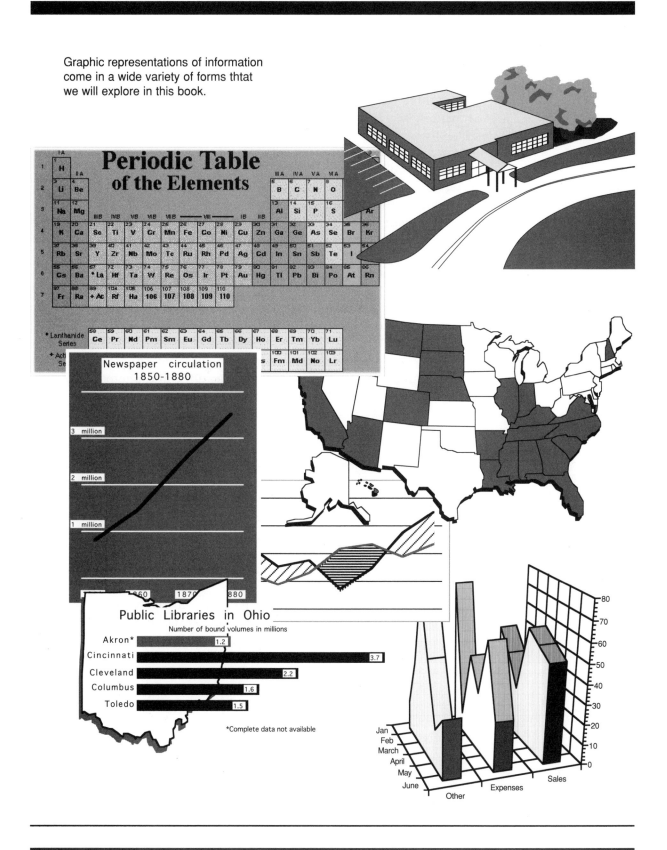

Public Libraries in Ohio
Number of bound volumes in millions

Akron*   1.2
Cincinnati   3.7
Cleveland   2.2
Columbus   1.6
Toledo   1.5

*Complete data not available

mation than at any time in our lifetime. Like most "revolutions," this change has come upon us rather suddenly and has both its up and down sides. The revolution deserves a few observations as we begin our examination and education about informational graphics.

Graphics allow us to present information that we could not present otherwise. How do you show readers an earthquake? You can describe the sensations that occurred when experiencing an earthquake. You can photograph the effects of the earthquake. But can you show them an earthquake?

When a major earthquake disrupted life in northern California in October 1989, a number of newspapers tried to show readers how the earthquake occurred and moved through the ground. They did this by creating a graphic that led readers through the process of the earthquake.

Using the same principles but working at a different level, a newspaper cannot photograph a car crash with multiple impacts. It can certainly run dramatic pictures of the aftermath of such a crash, but it cannot show with photographs the sequence of the crash. A well-drawn graphic can show how the crash occurred and what its sequence of events was.

Graphic presentation can bring information to readers that more "traditional" methods, e.g. the paragraph, headline and photograph, cannot deliver. Graphics can be used to explain and show to readers why and how things occur. The development of such graphics increases demands on the skills and creativity of journalists, however.

Graphics allow journalists to show the relationships of numerical data. One of the oldest pieces of advice directed toward improving writing is to "show, don't tell." Informational graphics allow us to take that advice literally. We can, in fact, show readers something rather than just tell them. We can allow them to draw their own conclusions about information – conclusions that we had once drawn for them.

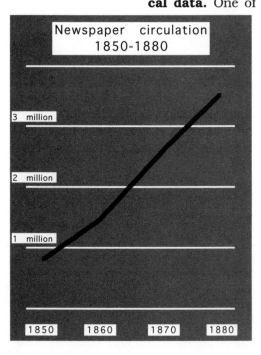

The graph on this page illustrates this point. It traces the rise of newspaper circulation during the middle of the 19th century. It presents information that could be fairly easily presented in paragraph form. The reader who looks at the graph, however, would be able to see that not only did newspaper circulation rise during that period, but that the rise was a steady trend after 1860. While the reader could be told this, the presentation is much more effective in visual than in paragraph form.

One of the great strengths of good graphic presentation is a graphic's ability to allow readers to make their own discoveries and conclusions about informa-

Sidebar

DEADLINES AND THE GRAPHIC JOURNALIST

Jack Smith

While graphic journalists may have several weeks to develop charts and graphs for in-depth news features, they often must produce art on an hour's notice.

"We scramble around for breaking news stories just like reporters do," Earnest Hart, graphics director at the Jackson (Miss.) *Clarion-Ledger,* said. "If we have three hours, we can produce a much more elaborate graphic than if we only have one hour. Deadlines are important because we have to adjust our efforts based on how much time we have."

Deadlines are always tight at the *Knoxville* (Tenn.) *News-Sentinel*, according to Dan Proctor, Sentinel art director.

"Reporters and editors here bring in assignments at different times every day," Proctor said. "Our deadlines are usually tight, especially on breaking stories."

Proctor attends daily news meetings at 3:30 p.m. Plans for the next day are finalized, and the Sentinel's three-man art staff works quickly to meet the 9 p.m. deadline.

Editors expecting elaborate charts or graphs learn adequate notice is crucial, Proctor added.

"The more time we have to review the information and work with the writers, the better."

Involving the writers in the idea stage also improves the work of the art and news departments, Proctor said.

"When the writer is involved in the art process, it helps them realize significant aspects of the story. When we tell a writer that we can't do a pie chart with the information they provide because it doesn't add up to 100 percent, that mistake doesn't slide by in the chart or the story. Otherwise, the writer might never know that."

tion. A journalist may not be aware of all the important relationships in a numerical graph or may not be able to point all of them out. A reader has the option of spending enough time with a graph to make those discoveries alone, and such discoveries become all the more important to the reader.

Graphics allow another way for editors to enliven a page. We have known for years that a page full of small type is not visually appealing. More appealing is the page whose type is broken up with headlines and pictures. Graphics not only offer an editor another way of presenting information, but they present a different visual cue for the reader. They concentrate ink on various parts of the page, thus stopping the eye of the reader, at least for a moment, and presenting the reader with information in a different form. Graphics give the reader more reason to stay with a publication.

Graphics give editors a means of presenting a large amount of information to the reader. A good graphic is "data rich." That is, there is a lot of information efficiently packaged into a small area. The best graphics are designed so that the more the reader looks at them, the more information they give. A reader may choose to spend only a few seconds with a graphic, in which case he or she will get the main idea of the graphic. If the reader spends more time with the graphic, he or she will find different levels of information.

At a purely visual level, graphics draw the attention of readers to information. Just as a large headline will indicate that editors believe information is particularly important, information in graphic form will also send a message to readers that the information contained within the graphic should be attended to. The color, artwork, and originality in design can serve to capture the reader's attention for information that might otherwise be missed.

Graphics allow publications to provide information to readers that may not be directly related to the presentation of news itself. One of the best examples of this indirect education of the readers is the locator map that sometimes accompanies news stories. The *Clarion-Ledger* in Jackson, Mississippi, has taken this idea one step further by building its world news page around a map of the world, its national news page around a map of the United States, and its state news page around a map of Mississippi. Each story on these pages is linked to a point on the map where it is located. The *Clarion-Ledger* has created this format to help its readers set the information on the page into a geographic context. (See the illustration in chapter 4.)

A map drawn by the Greek astronomer Ptolemy in the second century represents his knowledge and speculation about the shape of the world's land masses.

THE DEVELOPMENT OF INFOGRAPHICS

Infographics have existed from the times in which cavemen and women decided to represent their stories on the walls of their homes. They predate words and what we know today as "writing." Humans have always understood the need to represent information in a variety of ways to make it understandable and palatable, and this is particularly the case with numerical information. Some 5,000 years ago, the Egyptians developed the first calendar that divided time into 365 days for a year. Ancient astronomers drew intricate maps of their observations – observations they could describe in words but could better represent with pictures. Closer to earth, the Egyptians drew maps of the earth to chart such very real events as the flooding of the Nile River.

A history of infographics ought to mention Leonardo da Vinci, not because he was an innovator in this area, but because he is a precursor of the idea of infographics as they are being used today. The Italian renaissance genius kept hundreds of pages of journals in which he recorded his observations and thoughts about a wide variety of subjects. (Leonardo wrote backwards in these journals because he feared people would steal his ideas.) Leonardo was also an artist with a deft hand, and he realized that in explaining things to himself, words by themselves were often inadequate. These drawings – "graphics," if you will – appear on any

Leonardo da Vinci

Leonardo's notebooks and journals are filled with drawings and text intertwined. He mixed his artistic ability with his scientific curiosity to produce studies such as the one at the right on an astounding variety of subjects.

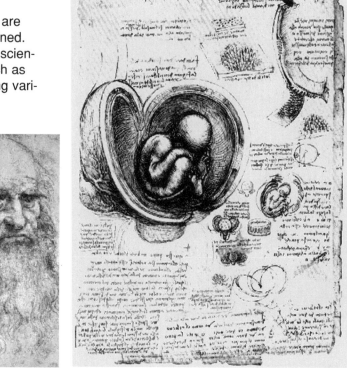

part of the page in which he felt they were necessary. He flowed his text beside them and around them. Da Vinci drew and wrote as ideas came to him, and he tried to represent the information he had in any way that made sense. He used a graphic if a graphic was called for, and it is these drawings that make the pages of his journal fascinating reading even today.

More directly affecting the development of today's charts and graphs was the work of French philosopher and scientist René Descartes, who lived during the first half of the 17th century. One of Descartes' many achievements was the development of a system of analytic geometry. He used numbers to describe the position of a point on a surface and developed a system of horizontal and vertical intersecting lines known as a Cartesian grid. This grid allowed scientists to "plot" statistical information, and it forms the basis of many of the charts and graphs that we use today.

While the history of charts and graphs has many famous contributors, one man – whose name is almost unknown to us – stands out as having the most direct influence on the way that charts and graphs appear today. That man is William Playfair, a Scottish-born writer and scientist born in 1759. Playfair gathered political and economic information in as systematic a way as he could for the time in which he lived, and in 1786 published a book entitled *The Commercial and Political Atlas.*

William Playfair

Playfair is rightly considered the father of modern infographics because of his development of the graphic forms we use today to present numerical information. The chart to the right shows English imports and exports to and from North America; today it would be called a ribbon chart (see chapter 3). The chart below is the first bar chart Playfair developed. He did not consider it successful because of some lack of data, but he set the standard for the form of bar charts to come.

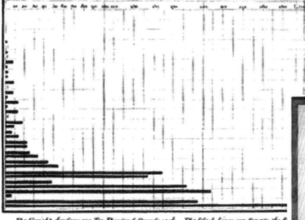

The chart to the right is the first to use a circle divided into parts from the center – what we know of today as the pie chart. It first appeared in a book by Playfair in 1805.

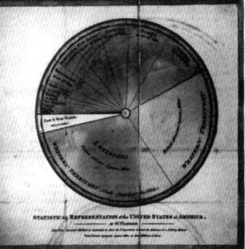

Included in this book were 44 charts, most of which plotted information over time. They were the first line or fever charts used to represent this kind of information. One of these charts used bars extending horizontally across the page to present information about Scotland's imports and exports.

In explaining why he developed this graphic representation, Playfair wrote: "The advantage proposed by those charts is not of giving a more accurate statement than by figures, but it is to give a more simple and permanent idea of the graduate progress and comparative amounts, at different periods, by presenting to the eye a figure, the proportions of which correspond with the amount of the sums intended to be expressed." In 1801, Playfair published a book in which circles represented amounts, and in 1805 he published another book in which a circle is divided with lines extending from the center. Thus, the pie chart was born. From Playfair's works come the three basic types of charts that we use today to present numerical data – line charts, bar charts, and pie charts.

Others followed Playfair in his use of graphics to present "to the eye" information that might not be as easily described. One of the most striking graphics of the 19th century was done by Charles Joseph Minard, a French engineer, who in 1861 plotted the progress and dissipation of Napoleon's army when it invaded Russia in 1812. The chart brilliantly plots six variables: the size of the army, its location, the direction of its movement, the time of its movement, and the temperatures it encountered.

Despite the work of Playfair, Minard, and others during the 19th century, the infographic remained a largely unused device by journalists. Maps of the movements of the armies of the Civil War were published frequently in newspapers and magazines, but virtually no graphic representations of the grim statistics of the war – men killed and wounded, cost of financing the war, etc. – can be found. Editors in the 1800s were hindered by a lack of information, an absence of understanding of charts, and the physical difficulty of setting up a chart in the age of "hot type."

By the 20th century, many of the problems had been mitigated, but the most prevelent graphic representation was the map. The United States was drawn into the affairs of the world by many momentous

Charles Joseph Minard

Minard's 1861 plotting of the progress of Napoleon's army into Russia in 1812 and its dissolution in retreat is one of the finest creations in the history of infographics. It combines a large amount of data with an interesting presentation and has the ability to engage the viewer in its information.

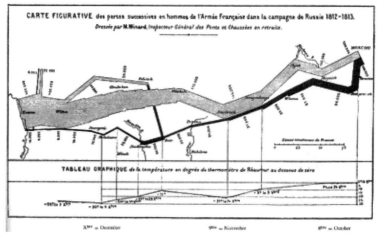

Sidebar

DEVELOPING AN AWARD-WINNING GRAPHIC

Jack Smith

The Jackson (Miss.) Clarion-Ledger's graphic recreation of the scene of Medgar Evers' 1963 murder won a Society of Newspaper Design Award of Excellence.

The graphic integrated a locator map, a street map, and a three-dimensional floor plan of Evers' home. Earnest Hart, graphics director at the Clarion-Ledger, said the project was a genuine team effort.

"We visited the murder site and shot reference photos, interviewed neighbors, and studied police records of the incident," Hart said.

The most challenging part of the project involved creating a three-dimensional sketch of the house from a two-dimensional floor plan.

"We took the floor plan and added walls to the house by creating upward and downward projections in Aldus Freehand," Hart said.

Evers, a civil rights activist, was murdered in his driveway in June 1963. Byron De La Beckwith was charged with the murder, but not convicted in two separate trials in 1964.

Thirty years later, Beckwith was brought back to Mississippi and tried again. (This time he was convicted.) This graphic was printed along with news stories of Beckwith's return to Mississippi.

The graphic was successful, Hart said, because it did more than duplicate facts in the story.

"Good graphics tell the reader what happened more quickly and effectively than a story can. This graphic worked because it did more than duplicate information."

For any graphic to be meaningful, Hart added, the information being presented should complement the accompanying news story.

events, including World War I and World War II, and the use of maps to help inform readers about these events was widespread. It was not until the late 1960s and early 1970s, however, that many editors realized the advantages of charts and graphs to present information. This was the era of "cold type," and it was easier for publications to create and reproduce these types of graphics.

The startup of *USA Today* in 1982 by the Gannett chain of newspapers legitimized the use of graphics in a way that revolutionized the newspaper industry. That newspaper made more and better use of graphics than had any paper in history. It used color brilliantly. It developed a style of integrating a graphic with a drawing – called a chartoon – that editors hoped would enlighten and entertain the reader. The paper took the idea of the weather map and blew it up to half a page and covered it with color and information. While many critics have vehmently chastised *USA Today* for its many sins and mistakes, there is little doubt that it has had a more profound effect on the profession of journalism than any other publication of the second half of this century.

DISADVANTAGES OF GRAPHICS

Infographics are not perfect vehicles for presenting information. They have their disadvantages, particularly to those who produce publications on very tight deadlines, and these disadvantages should not be ignored.

To begin with, informational graphics take a great deal of time and talent to produce. Computer hardware and software have greatly accelerated the production in some cases, but computers do not produce graphics. People do; and those people must have the time and talent to do this properly. Many editors, believing that graphs spring fully grown from special software, do not realize the amount of time that is required for even the simplest graphic form. One graphics editor recently said he always attempts to estimate the time that it will take a graphic journalist on his staff to complete an assignment for an editor. "I want the editors to understand that these things are not automatic," he said.

Time is one thing; talent is another. Graphic journalists must understand the rudiments of the conventions and design of graphics as well as the operation of computer hardware and software. Ideally, they should also be trained journalists who understand news and information. They should be people who understand sources of information, and the importance of accuracy. Many graphic journalists, however, have not been trained in traditional journalistic practices. The field of graphic journalism is continuing to emerge, and most journalism programs pay little attention to this important area. Despite this lack of formal training, the field has developed many excellent graphic journalists who understand both graphic forms and journalistic practices. Many of those journalists work at publications willing to commit time and resources to developing people in these areas.

Another disadvantage of graphics is that they can be easily distorted. The development of a graphic is not automatic. Many informed choices have to be made when they are being put together, and those choices must be made by people who understand both the information and the form that is being used.

Mistakes and distortions can during each part of this development process. The distortions are rarely deliberate, but they do occur, and often the editing process of the publication is not designed to offer the proper checks on graphs. Editors may understand words and paragraphs completely, but they may not fully understand the conventions and forms of graphic information. They may not even understand fully what information should and should not be presented in graphic form.

Still another disadvantage of graphics is that they may be distracting rather than informative to the readers. Many readers, having seen more charts and graphs in most of the publications they read, have developed some understanding of graphics. Still, journalists should be careful in their presentation of information to make sure that the information – not the form – promotes understanding rather than confusion among the readers.

DO GRAPHICS HELP THE READER?

Do graphic forms help the reader to retain and understand information?

Most people who deal with these forms believe that they do. "People will look at pictures," Jan White, an author who has written extensively in this area, has said. Yet the research that has been done on questions

In 1994 when a young American was sentenced to be caned by Singapore authorities, the government in Singapore came under heavy criticism for this form of punishment. As a way of defending itself, a government publication produced this infographic on the caning procedure.

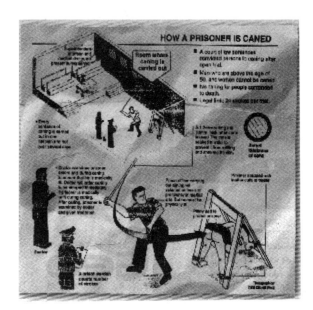

relating to retention and understanding of graphic information is decidedly mixed. To date, this research has not produced clearcut answers on what graphic forms work the best or even if they work at all.

Several reasons could explain why research does not yet "prove" that graphics work. One is that modern research in this area is not abundant. The resurgence of graphic forms in journalistic publications was not based on research about what readers wanted or needed. Rather, it was driven for the most part by the technology that suddenly became available to journalists in the 1980s to produce graphic forms. As more research is conducted, we can hope that a clearer picture will emerge about what graphic forms have what effects.

Another consideration of the current lack of research support for the saliency of graphics is that research methods may not be sensitive enough to pick up the effects of graphics. Scholars are constantly working to develop ways to detect the effects of graphics in experimental subjects.

As mentioned earlier, despite this lack of research, many continue

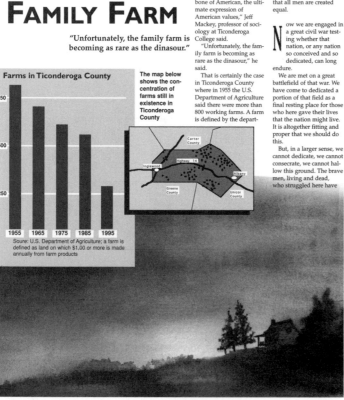

SUNSET ON THE FAMILY FARM

"Unfortunately, the family farm is becoming as rare as the dinasour."

Family farms in Ticoderoga County have been dwinding steadily for more than 40 years now, and agricultural officials say there is no comeback in sight.

"Our image is that the family farm is the backbone of American, the ultimate expression of American values," Jeff Mackey, professor of sociology at Ticonderoga College said.

"Unfortunately, the family farm is becoming as rare as the dinasour," he said.

That is certainly the case in Ticonderoga County where in 1955 the U.S. Department of Agriculture said there were more than 800 working farms. A farm is defined by the depart-

ment as land on which $1,000 worth of farm produce was made or could have been mad during the year.our score and seven years ago, our fathers brought forth on this continent a new nation, conceived in liberty and dedicated to the proposition that all men are created equal.

Now we are engaged in a great civil war testing whether that nation, or any nation so conceived and so dedicated, can long endure.

We are met on a great battlefield of that war. We have come to dedicated a portion of that field as a final resting place for those who here gave their lives that the nation might live. It is altogether fitting and proper that we should do this.

But, in a larger sense, we cannot dedicate, we cannot consecrate, we cannot hallow this ground. The brave men, living and dead, who struggled here have

Farms in Ticonderoga County

750
500
250

1955 1965 1975 1985 1995

Soure: U.S. Department of Agriculture; a farm is defined as land on which $1.00 or more is made annually from farm products

The map below shows the concentration of farms still in existence in Ticonderoga County

Carter County
Highway 14
Inglewood
Albany
Greene County
Unicoi County

This page demonstates a number of the graphic forms that will be discussed in subsequent chapters of the book, including charts, maps, illustrations, and type-based graphics.

Chapter review and highlights

The graphics revolution
- Graphics allow journalists to present information they could not otherwise present
- Graphics can show relationships
- Graphics can enliven a page
- Graphics can be space efficient, presenting a great deal of information in a small space
- Graphics draw the attention of the reader

Developers of infographics
Leonardo da Vinci, who mixed text and graphics in his journals

René Descartes, who developed the grid system of analytic geometry

William Playfair, the father of infographics, who first used charts to represent numerical data

Disadvantages of graphics
- The require time and talent
- They can be easily distorted
- They can be distracting rather than informative

What was odd about the way Leonardo wrote in his journals?

What newspaper sparked the "graphics revolution" discussed in this chapter?

Coming up:
Chapter 2: Principles of graphic presentation; what does it take to make a good graphic

Chapter 3: Chart-based graphics; bar, line and pie charts.

to feel – often very strongly – that graphic forms for presenting information do indeed help the reader. That belief has been prevalent for many years. Leonardo da Vinci thought that. Many of his journals show that da Vinci integrated graphics with words naturally and seemingly effortlessly. When da Vinci felt that words could suffice to express his thought, he used them. When he had an idea that could be better expressed as a graphic, he often integrated that graphic into his text.

The advent of printing technology and the strictures of type forced us to separate words and graphics. Because type was easier to produce, words prevailed. Graphics, when used at all, were often relegated to decorations on the page – elements that could break up the type but that contributed little to the meanings of the words.

Today's technology has brought us full circle. With today's computer software, we are able to create graphics and to integrate them with words as easily as Leonardo did. Many journalists feel passionately that we should take advantage of this opportunity of reintroducing graphics to ourselves and our readers as a form of presentation of information that is worthy of our best talents and efforts. By making themselves more graphically literate, journalists can better inform their readers and help them understand a complex, mystifying and interesting world.

FURTHER READING

Mark Feeney, "Beyond the Voodoo stick," *Design,* Apr/May /June, 1994, p. 6.

Howard Finberg and Brue Itule, *Visual Editing: A Graphic Guide for Journalists,* Belmont, Calif.: Wadsworth, 1990.

Nigel Holmes, *Designer's Guide to Creating Charts and Diagrams,* New York: Watson Guptill, 1991.

Matthew P. Murgio, *Communications Graphics,* New York: Van Nostrand Reinhold Co., 1969.

Edward Smith and Donna Hajash. "Informational Graphics in 30 Daily Newspapers," *Journalism Quarterly,* 1988, 714-718.

Edward Tufte, *Envisioning Information,* Cheshire, Conn.: Graphics Press, 1990.

Edward Tufte, *The Visual Display of Quantative Information,* Cheshire, Conn.: Graphics Press, 1983.

Sandra Utt and Steve Pasternack, "Use of graphic devices in a competitive siutation: a case study of ten cities," *Newspaper Research Journal,* 1985, 7-16.

Sandra Utt and Steve Pasternack, "How they look: An updated study of America's newspaper front pages," *Journalism Quarterly,* 1989, 621-627.

2

Principles of graphic presentation

Composition is finding and
portraying variety within unity.
PLATO

raphic presentation is an integral and necessary part of the information formats used by publications today. Graphics are neither decorations nor afterthoughts. For certain types of information, they are the best means of telling the reader information that the publication wants to transmit. For this reason, all journalists should have an understanding of what graphics are and how they should be used. This understanding begins with a knowledge of some of the basic principles of design.

The design principles discussed in this chapter specifically relate to informational graphics and their use in modern journalism. Much has been written about the many facets of visual design for both artistic and informational purposes, and students interested in this area have a wide variety of sources they can go to for additional information and discussion. In this chapter, we will confine our discussion to those principles that will be useful to the development of informational graphics and which will help in understanding other parts of this book.

Reading order

This graph draws the eye of the reader to the lower right. Once there, the reader must then travel back to the upper right to get the information the graph has to offer.

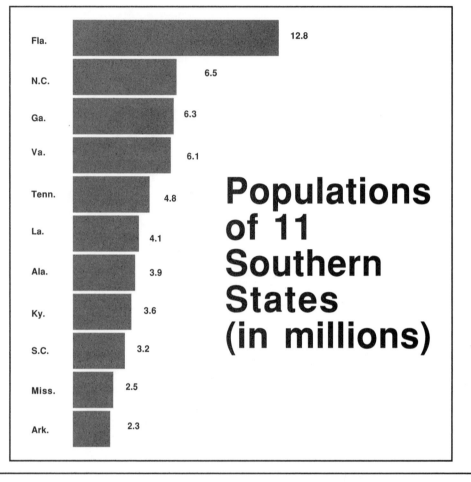

Fla.	12.8
N.C.	6.5
Ga.	6.3
Va.	6.1
Tenn.	4.8
La.	4.1
Ala.	3.9
Ky.	3.6
S.C.	3.2
Miss.	2.5
Ark.	2.3

Populations of 11 Southern States (in millions)

DESIGN PRINCIPLES Some design principles exist because of the structure of the language and the conventions that have been developed over many centuries about how ideas and information should be communicated. Others have developed because of the physical structure of the eye and the visual sense of humans and the way they see and process information. Both types of principles are presented in this section.

Most people have some knowledge and understanding of these principles, even though they may not be specifically aware of them. One of the basic principles of design is the following:

Reading normally occurs from left to right and from top to bottom. This principle is obvious, but it is important for anyone involved in design to remember. The tendency of left-to-right, top-to-bottom reading and viewing is so prevalent that it seems natural. Viewers of the printed page will begin at the upper left corner of the page.

This tendency does not obligate the designer to start a design in the upper left corner of a section or page. Readers will begin their viewing elsewhere if given a reason to do so. That reason might be a brightly colored picture in the middle of a newspaper page or a strong, dark headline on the right side of the page. Designers need to be aware of the times when they violate this left-to-right, top-to-bottom principle. Violations should be handled with care and with an understanding of the consequences. For instance, the graph on the next page has the headline to the right of the graph. The headline is darker than the graph and more likely to catch the reader's attention first, rather than the graph. Once the reader looks at the headline, where will he or she go?

There is nothing wrong with constructing a graph in this way as long as the graphic journalist is aware of what he or she is doing. Giving this kind of emphasis to the headline – or any other element of the graph – may be perfectly appropriate, but it should be what the journalist means to do. It should not happen accidentally.

Focus and contrast are particularly important design elements for the graphic journalist. In this instance, focus means a concentration of ink or color so that the eye of the reader is drawn to that point. In the graph on the previous page, the eye is drawn to the headline because it has the most ink concentrated in that area.

Not only does the headline have a lot of black ink concentrated in one area, but it also draws the eye because the area around it is white. This combination of very light and very dark is called contrast. Contrast is one way for the graphic journalist to make sure that readers see what the journalist wants them to see.

On page 22 there are three versions of the same graph used on the previous page. The one on the left has the same gray area to represent each of the states. On the right, the journalist has decided that the readers should take notice of the population of Tennessee in particular. The journalist has done this by putting the bar that represents Tennessee in a darker ink. Readers may look at the entire chart and may even seek out other states, but their eyes will inevitably be drawn to the bar that represents Tennessee because of its contrasting nature.

Graphics should achieve a balance among its elements that invites the reader into the graphic and that guides the reader through it. The design principle of balance means that the size of elements should not be out of proportion to their importance to the graphic itself. The elements should be clearly delineated. If elements overlap, they should do so for a purpose and should not obscure important information. While the placement of elements might guide a reader through the graphic, the reader should also be able to browse or scan.

The best way for anyone to develop a sense of balance for graphic forms is to study closely informational graphics wherever they appear.

This examination should be accompanied by questions about the size and placement of elements and a judgment about what works and what does not work. It would be a disservice to the profession to reduce balance to a set of "correct" formulas that are most pleasing to the author. The possibilities of graphic journalism are too broad for that to be useful. Individual graphic journalists should use their imagination and creativity within the discipline of generally accepted forms and customs that are discussed later in this chapter.

Graphics should have a unity that draws attention to the information they are presenting and away from their design. Elements in a graphic should work together rather than competing with one another. What this usually means is that a graphic should have a small number of type fonts (only one, if possible) and contrasting shades or colors.

Once again, on the previous page we have used the population graph to illustrate the point. The graph measures only one thing – the

Contrast and emphasis

The graph on the left treats all of the data equally and lets the reader decide what to emphasize. In the middle graph, the eye is drawn immediately to the bar representing Tennessee because it is darker than the other bars. Its difference from the other bars gives it emphasis. The graph on the right unnecessarily uses too many different patterns – something that is easy to do with the computer. The result is confusion for the reader.

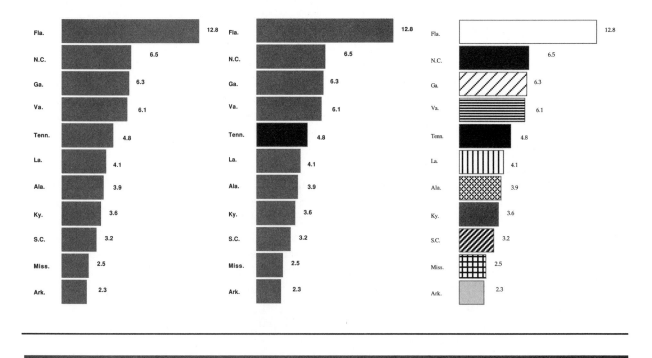

White space

All of the lines on the right are the same size. In the first set, no line is distinguishable from the other. In the second, however, the fifth line is easily distinguishable because there is more white space around it than around the other lines. The proper use of white space can help set off items that the designer wants to emphasize for the reader.

White space (or empty space) in a graphic must be used wisely. Elements in a graphic should be fitted together so that there is neither too much nor too little white space. The graphic below is found in chapter 4 as an illustration for another point made there, but here it serves to show how the designer fit the elements together for an effective use of white space. The graphic on the left treats each element separately and gives it a separate horizontal space. The one on the right integrates the elements by taking advantage of their shapes to fit them together. The graphic still contains plenty of white space so that it is pleasing to the eye of the reader.

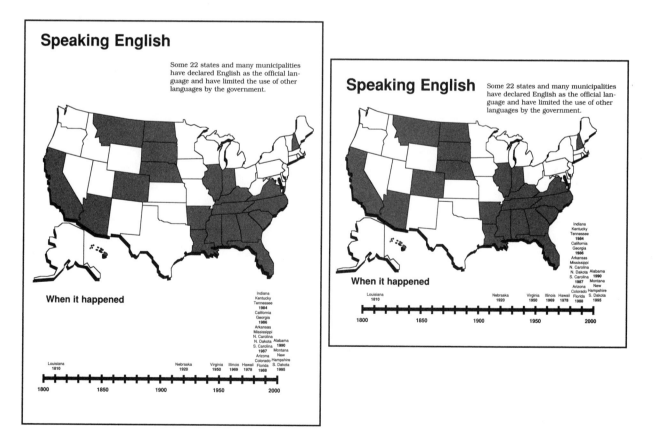

Choosing the right form

Information can often be represented in a variety of ways. It is up to the graphic journalist to choose the form that best fits the data and allows the journalist to make a point with it

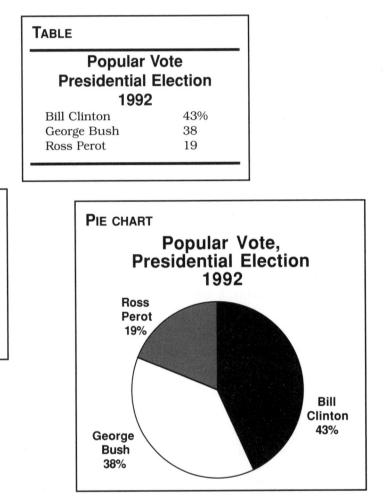

TABLE

Popular Vote
Presidential Election
1992

Bill Clinton	43%
George Bush	38
Ross Perot	19

PARAGRAPH

Bill Clinton received 43 percent of the popular vote for the presidency in 1992, while George Bush got 38 percent and Ross Perot got 19 percent.

PIE CHART

Popular Vote,
Presidential Election
1992

Ross Perot 19%

Bill Clinton 43%

George Bush 38%

population of each state. Consequently, it is not necessary to have the parts representing each state in different shadings, such as in the graph to the right. Nor is it necessary to have different type fonts to represent the headlines and the names of the states and the population figures. All of these different elements compete with one another for the reader's attention and thus detract from the information that the graphic is supposed to present.

Purpose and content, rather than form, should drive the creation of the graphic. Today's graphic journalist has many powerful tools at his or her disposal. Combined with some talent and imagination, these

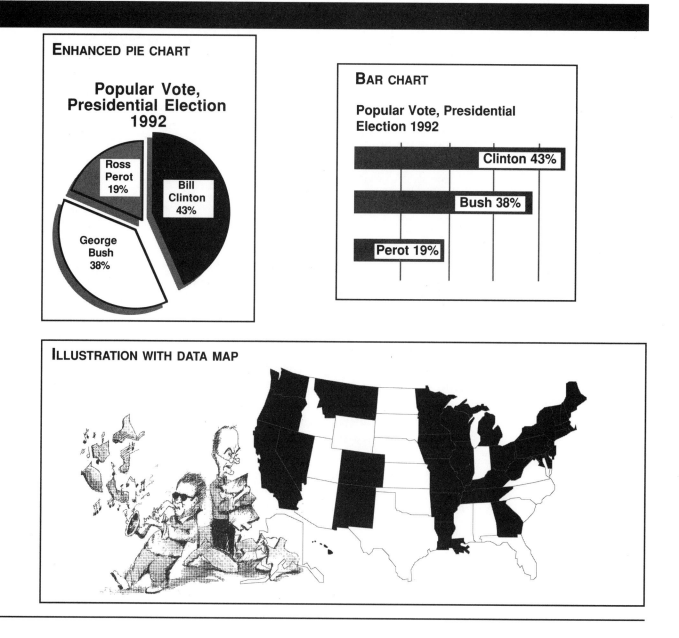

ENHANCED PIE CHART

Popular Vote, Presidential Election 1992

Ross Perot 19%

Bill Clinton 43%

George Bush 38%

BAR CHART

Popular Vote, Presidential Election 1992

Clinton 43%

Bush 38%

Perot 19%

ILLUSTRATION WITH DATA MAP

tools enable the journalist to create slick, eye-catching graphics that can dazzle editors and readers alike.

But how far should the graphic journalist go in using these tools? The journalist should always ask the questions, "What is the purpose of what I am doing?" and "What is necessary to accomplish that purpose?"

Consider the graphics on these two pages, beginning first with the paragraph of information. The paragraph states rather simply what the information is. The table gives this same information in a non-paragraph form. The pie chart, which in the hands of an experienced graphic journalist took about five minutes to create, presents this information in a straightforward but graphic way. The enhanced pie chart took more time to create – about 15 minutes – and is more likely to capture the attention of the reader. Finally, the illustration using the outline of the United States and the drawings of the candidates took a good part of the working day for a talented illustrator to produce, and it certainly gives the reader some entertainment as well as some information.

In each case, the purpose of the graphic is different, even though the information is the same. Editors and journalists need to have a good idea of why they are presenting information. The purpose and content of the information should combine to help the journalist decide what is the best form for the information.

CONVENTIONS OF GRAPHICS

Graphic forms have been in use since the times that cave dwellers drew pictures on their walls to tell stories. In modern times, the graphic forms that we are most familiar with have been developed over several centuries. These forms are used within certain conventions or customs that are generally accepted by those who create informational graphics. The purpose of these graphic conventions is to establish some understandings between the developer of the graphic and the reader on what the graphic represents. Just as journalistic writers and editors have style rules, graphic journalists have expectations that are not all that different from the general rules of writing.

The first and most important convention is the adherence to accuracy. The information in a graphic should be accurate to whatever standard is acceptable to the publication. Information should be correct, up-to-date and presented within a proper context. Grammar and spelling should be correct. All of the other normal procedures for ensuring accuracy of information should be followed by the graphic journalist.

Another convention that must be strictly observed is that the form of the graphic should be appropriate for the data or information that is being presented. This convention is particularly important in working with numerical data. Certain graphic forms are appropriate for certain types of data and are most inappropriate for other types of data. These forms and their appropriateness will be discussed more completely in Chapter 3. Understanding these forms and their appropriateness for data is essential.

When graphic forms are used to represent numerical data, the presentation should be physically proportional. Strictly speaking, in the graph concerning populations of states used earlier in this chapter, the bar representing Florida, which has a population of 12.8 million, should be slightly more than twice as long as that representing Georgia, which has a population of 6.3 million.

This convention is violated with surprising regularity in graphs presented in magazines and newspapers. Many times, the violations occur because the graphic journalists do not understand the data they are trying to represent. Sometimes, graphic journalists violate this convention because they want to emphasize a larger point than the individual items of data that are in a graph.

The idea of proportionality is sometimes subtle and difficult to understand. Proportionality is easiest to achieve when there is only one dimension involved in the objects that must be proportional. The graph of population figures below is a simple bar chart, so representing the populations of the various states with different sizes of bars is a seemingly simple matter. If the area of the bar represented the population, the bar representing Florida would have to be twice as big as the bar representing Georgia, as in the top part of the example to the right. Generally, we do not construct charts in this way because they are not particularly pleas-

Proportionality

In most graphics that represent numerical data, proportionality is achieved by using only one dimension of the figure that represents the data. In the top graph, both dimensions are used to achieve proportionality. In the other, only one – the length along the imaginary x-axis – is used. The second graph is the more conventional use. Problems with proportionality often occur when the designer of the graphic is working with two-dimensional figures. If the designer had used only one dimension to represent the barrels, the data would have made the figures look less like barrels and more like tubes. As it is, however, the figures have lost much of their representational quality because they are not in proportion to one another. The designer probably should have used bars on a two-dimensional grid.

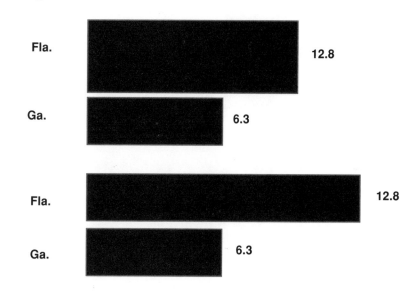

Price of a barrel of imported oil

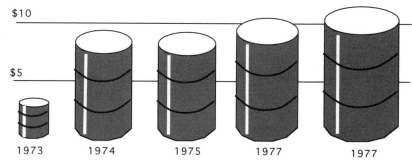

Depth

The subject of depth in infographics can be a controversial one for graphic journalists. Computer applications make depth easy to achieve when building graphics. Depth can easily distort or obscure data when that is not the intention of the journalist. The major reason for adding a depth function to a graphic is to gain the attention of the reader and to make a visual impression. This reason may not be strong enough to offset the dangers that are inherent in using it, however. Graphic journalists should use extreme caution when considering whether or not to add a third dimension to their graphics.

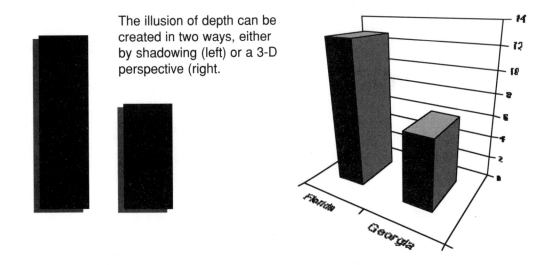

The illusion of depth can be created in two ways, either by shadowing (left) or a 3-D perspective (right.

ing to the eye. Rather, in the lower part, we have two bars whose widths represent the populations of the states.

Whenever a third dimension is introduced or when objects are taken off a flat plane, the problem of achieving proportionality becomes more difficult. Here we encounter both depth and perspective, two elements that make an object appear to be three dimensional. Depth means adding a side or two to the objects in a graph to make them appear as if they are coming off the page. (Computer graphing programs contain a function that will add depth automatically to most objects that it creates.) *Depth does nothing to make a graph more accurate since the elements in a graph rarely represent actual objects.* Depth often diminishes the true proportionality of the objects in a graph because it moves them away from a background scale that readers use to measure them. On the other hand, depth can make a graph more attention-getting and more interesting to look at.

The element of depth also means that graphic journalists must deal with perspective. Perspective is an artistic technique that controls the viewpoint of the viewer toward the graphic. Perspective is based on the

A primer on projection

Picturing a chart in three-dimensions on a two-dimensional surface is a popular technique for many graphic journalists. Technically, this technique has three types: axonometric, oblique, and perspective, all of which are illustrated on this page.

Axonometric projection shows three faces of an object, with the projection angles on each side extending equally from a projection plane.

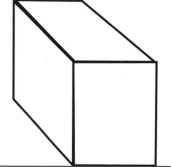

Oblique projection shows three faces of an object but with one face parallel to a projection plane.

Perspective projection (below) comes closest to the way that we really see three-dimensional objects. This project is based on the fact that the farther objects are away from us, the smaller they appear. This also applies to different sides of an object so that they are drawn smaller than what they really are. Perspective projection uses the concept of a **vanishing point.** That means that if straight lines were extended far enough from each side of an object, they would eventually cross as some point.

This drawing shows parallel perspective, which means that one side is parallel to the projection plane. The object to the right shows angular perspective, which means there is more than one vanishing point.

Sidebar

THE GOOD GRAPHIC: TIPS FROM THE PROS

Jack Smith

A good informational graphic does more than decorate a page. It tells a story of its own.

While a graphic does break up "gray matter" on a news page, its true benchmark is its ability to effectively and accurately communicate to viewers some significant information.

The following are a few "tricks of the trade" from graphics journalists working in the field.

Earnest Hart, graphics director at the *Jackson* (Miss.) *Clarion-Ledger:*

"A good graphic can tell a story more quickly and accurately than a print story."

Hart's tips:
- *Accuracy* - If it's not right, it's a failure.
- *Subtle color tones* - Too much color can be counterproductive.
- *Organization* - Composition should be clean and not crowded.

Dan Proctor, graphics director at *The Knoxville (Tenn.) News Sentinel:*

"First of all, you must have information that is significant, and it must be correct."

Proctor's tips:
- *It starts with the head* - Before producing the graphic, write a terse, informative headline and sub-head. It's critical for the reader, and for the artist transforming an idea into a graphic.
- *Bold lines, eye-catching colors* - Draw the viewer's attention to the graphic's most important element with color saturation and bold lines at the points of emphasis.

- *Avoid graphics for the sake of graphics* - Unless you can show an increase, decrease, or a significant trend, a graphic won't show much.

Scott Davis, graphic artist at the *Ithaca (N.Y.) Journal* (circulation 19,000)

"To be successful, you have to approach graphics as another way of telling the story. Graphics aren't simply decorations."

Davis' tips:
- *Don't repeat the story, add to it* - Use information graphics to add details not included in the story.
- *Create a single dominant image* - The most important element in the graphic should be the largest.
- *Be clever with the copy* - Copy accompanying a graphic should do more than simply describe it.

Brad Diller, illustrator at the *Nashville Banner* (formerly at *The Charleston [W.Va.] Daily Mail)*

"To produce a good illustration, you must first consider how conducive the subject matter is to illustration."

Diller's tips:
- *Start with a theme* - Before drawing an illustration, articulate the story's underlying emotional element or theme.
- *Write short, if at all* - Too much writing in an illustration dilutes its purpose.
- *Use color judiciously* - "Color overkill" can hinder color's eye-catching ability. Avoid use of color for the sake of color.

observation that the closer something is to us, the larger it is. As an object gets farther away, its actual size does not diminish, but our perception of it does. It will diminish to a vanishing point, where we cannot see it at all. The vanishing point is located along a horizon line.

Perspective also can diminish the proportionality of the elements of a graph, so that the objects of the graph do not actually represent numerically the values that the graph is trying to show. Consequently, many who have studied this field believe that depth and perspective should not be used. There are others, however, who argue that the use of depth and perspective makes the elements of a graph appear more realistic. As humans, they say, we do not view objects in the real world with exact proportionality. Consequently, graphs should be good representations of the information they are showing but should not be held to a high standard of proportionality.

TOWARD THE GOOD GRAPHIC

So far, this chapter has discussed some of the conventions and techniques that have come into use with modern informational graphics. We will end this chapter with a discussion of the development of the attitude or philosophy of the graphic journalist. Not only should the graphic journalist have a good grasp of the tools and techniques of the field, but he or she should also have some depth of understanding about what is to be accomplished with graphics.

Chapter review and highlights

Design principles
- Reading occurs from left-to-right, top-to-bottom
- Contrast in a graphic uses variations of light and dark for emphasis
- Balance among a graphic's elements guides the reader through the graphic and stresses proportionality
- Unity in a graphic is achieved by consistency in type styles and their usage
- White space must be carefully used to create a pleasing graphic

Choosing the right graphic form
Purpose and content should drive the creative process

Graphic conventions
- Graphic conventions establish an understanding between graphic developer and reader

- All normal journalistic procedures for ensuring accuracy should be followed in the creation of graphics
- The chosen form for a graphic must be appropriate for the data being presented
- When dealing with numerical data, presentation must be physically proportional
- Depth and perspective can enhance a graphic's appearance, but must be used carefully

Graphics should be "data rich"
Graphics should contain substantive information for the readers to browse through with ease

In the following chapters, four types of graphics will be discussed:
- Charts, maps, type, and illustrations

Calvin and Hobbes   by Bill Watterson

We can begin by talking about the relationship of the graphic journalist to the audience. A good journalist of any stripe has a healthy respect for the audience. This respect is particularly important in this age of graphics. Many people view graphics as a way of imparting information to people who could not understand it otherwise or are too lazy to read text. For journalists to take this view of their audience would be demeaning to the audience and the work that they do.

Graphics should be produced because they are the best way of gaining the attention of readers and helping them understand the information that is being presented. The fact that they may make the publication look better or that they are interesting for the journalists themselves to produce may also be considerations in their creation, but they are clearly secondary.

This respect for the audience should do away with the old bromide: "Graphics must be simple; otherwise, people won't read or understand them." Informational graphics do not have to be simple any more than news stories have to be simple. Informational graphics should be understandable, but that does not mean they should be simple. A graphic is often the best means of presenting rather complex information to the reader. As Edward Tufte writes in his book *Envisioning Information*, "Clutter and confusion are failures of design, not attributes of information. Often the less complex and less subtle the line, the more ambiguous and less interesting is the reading. Stripping the detail out of data is a style based on personal preference and fashion, considerations utterly indifferent to substantive content." (p. 51)

Tufte, who is one of the leading thinkers about informational graphics, argues that graphics should be "data rich." That is, graphics should have enough information in them – and should be designed in such a way – that readers can browse through them. The ideal graphic is one that allows the reader to make discoveries about the information that are not pointed out by the graphic journalist and not immediately apparent.

It is simply not true that readers glance at informational graphics and then look away anymore than it is true that readers glance at and then look away from headlines or pictures. Readers will take time to look at, read and study what is interesting to them. Interesting information that is attractively presented will find an audience.

CATEGORIZING INFOGRAPHICS In modern journalism, four major graphic elements exist: charts, maps, type, and illustrations. Charts are representations of numerical data that use conventional forms such as the bar chart or pie chart. Maps – which, like charts, are based on numerical data – represent location. Type is the set of symbols that make up text. Illustration is any sort of representational drawing.

In the following chapters of this book, we discuss four basic types of infographics based on these graphic elements: chart-based graphics, maps, type-based graphics, and illustration-based graphics. This categorization is not meant to suggest that these types of graphics are discreet. Each type of graphic may, and often does, use a variety of graphic elements. The purpose of this categorization is to give some order to our study of infographics and to help us understand how each of these graphic elements works and what purposes they can serve.

FURTHER READING

Bob Bohle, "What research tells us about graphics," *Design,* Apr/May /June, 1994, p. 32.

Barry Hollander, "Nespaper graphes and inadvertent persuasion," *Visual Communication Quarterly,* Winter 1994.

James D. Kelly, "The effects of display format and data density on time spent reading statistics in text, tables and graphs, *Journalism Quarterly,* Spring 1993.

Stephen Kosslyn, *Elements of Graph Design,* 1993.

Douglas B. Ward, "The effectiveness of side-bar graphics," *Journalism Quarterly,* Summer 1993.

3

Chart-based graphics

At the heart of quantitative reasoning is
a single question: *Compared to what?*
EDWARD TUFTE

Using numbers—counting things—is one of the ways in which society knows about itself. Our communities are so large and our interests so wide-ranging that we must reduce what we know about ourselves to numbers. That is simply the way we understand who we are and what is happening in our society. Because it is journalism's responsibility to tell society about itself, journalists must learn to handle the large variety of numbers that come their way. Charts are often an ideal way of presenting numerical information to readers.

Many journalists have a self-confessed aversion to numbers. Many say they never did well in mathematics courses, and that is why they are in journalism. They are more comfortable working with words than numbers. Despite this know-nothing attitude toward numbers, there is nothing particularly complex about the numbers that we use daily and about the numbers that interest us the most. We deal with all sorts of numbers

– from the percentage of the public that approves of the way the president is handling his job to the price of gasoline to the cost of a 30-second commercial during the Super Bowl. Numbers are a basic way of organizing our lives, and in many cases they fascinate us.

This chapter examines the conventions and techniques available to journalists for handling numbers and creating infographics.

REPRESENTING NUMERICAL DATA

Chart-based graphics present numerical information in a non-text form. These forms are likely to be proportional representations of the numbers themselves. These are what many people refer to when they talk about informational graphics.

Charts commonly serve two functions: to show amounts and to show relationships. They can often perform these functions more quickly and efficiently than words. Various types of charts have been developed to perform these functions, and this section will discuss the major types of charts commonly used by the mass media. The types of charts introduced here are what we might think of as basic charts. They have many variations and can sometimes be found in combinations that are useful in presenting information.

Chart-based graphics are highly popular in today's newspapers. Computer software makes them relatively easy to produce (as we shall see later in this chapter), and many people spend a lot of time gathering the information that can be presented in charts.

Graphic journalists must always abide by two principles when developing charts: accuracy and clarity.

Accuracy is always the chief goal of any journalist. The responsibilities of the graphic journalist for obtaining accurate information and presenting that information accurately are no less than they are for any other journalist. A graphic journalist should always check sources of information to make sure that they are the best available. The journalist should always question information to make sure that it is clear and complete. The graphic journalist must also understand the tools at his or her disposal in order to present information in the best form and context.

While accuracy refers to what a graphic journalist does with information, clarity refers to what the reader does with the information. The journalist must present the information he or she has in such a way that it is understandable and complete. Each part of a chart should be cleanly designed so that it does not confuse the reader.

In addition to the principles of accuracy and clarity, graphic journalists must consider a number of characteristics about charts during their development. The following are some of those characteristics:

Simplicity. By simplicity, we do not mean "dumbing down" graphics to meet some low expectation that we have of the audience's intelligence or their proclivity for understanding the information we have.

Graphic journalists should not be afraid to present complex information to their readers, but the appearance of the graphic itself should be uncluttered, and its purpose should be self-evident. One of the criticisms of many graphics is that they are "chartoons" – that is, they have too many little figures and drawings that do not add to the reader's understanding of the information in the graphic. Just as good writing contains no unnecessary words and phrases, a good graphic contains the minimum items necessary for understanding the information and the maximum items for good appearance.

Consistency. Publications often develop a graphics style just as they adopt a writing style. This style includes rules about what kind of type is used, when color is appropriate, how information is attributed, and a variety of other matters. Like style rules for writing, these rules help both the staff in producing graphics and the reader in understanding them. Consistency in appearance helps a publication establish a relationship with its readers, and makes reading more efficient.

Headlines. Oddly enough, one of the most difficult things about producing an informational graphic is writing its headline. Headlines for graphics do not have to follow the rules of headlines for articles; in most publications, they can simply be labels. They need to identify the central idea of the graphic, however, and this is difficult to do in just a few words. One approach many graphic journalists use in writing a headline for a graphic is to write it before the graphic is built. Doing that gives them the central idea to keep in mind while producing the graphic.

Attribution. Information in graphics should be attributed, just as information in news stories should be attributed. As with other information in a publication, sometimes the source is obvious and does not need to be specified. In other cases, attribution is vital to the understanding of a graphic.

Use of color. Charts lend themselves to color, and many publications use charts to showcase their ability to handle color. Color helps emphasize certain parts of the graphic; it also contributes to a pleasing appearance for the graphic. Color is easy to overuse, however, and editors should be careful that the use of color does not get in the way of the information in the chart.

ELEMENTS IN A CHART Charts contain a variety of elements that work together to help the reader understand the information in them. Not all charts contain all of the following elements, but each serves a specific function.

Headline. Headlines, discussed in the previous section, are important because they convey the central idea of the information contained within the chart. A headline may be a label (unless the style of the publication requires more); that is, they do not require a verb, and they need not relate specific information or an interpretation of that information to the reader.

Some graphic journalists advise that the headline should be the first thing that a journalist does in creating a chart. Writing the headline first helps the journalist understand exactly what information he or she is trying to convey.

Labels. Parts of a chart often need to be identified. These identifications are called labels and can be put on any element of a chart, although the graphic journalist should not label the obvious. Too many labels can be irritating and confusing.

Two of the most common labels in a chart are *categories* and *values*. Categories refer to the things that are being shown in a chart. Values are the amounts of the things being shown. Those who develop charts must

Elements in a chart

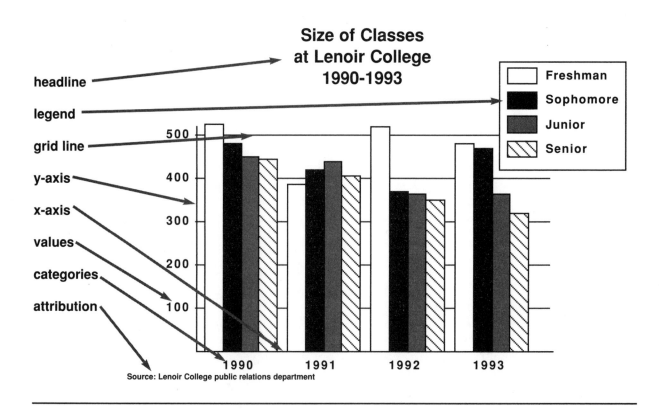

have a clear idea of the difference between a category and a value because graphing software requires that each be identified properly.

Axis. When bar, column or line charts are used, they require a horizontal and vertical line to establish the values and categories. The horizontal line is the *x-axis*. The vertical line is the *y-axis*. Which line represents the categories and which the values will depend on the type of chart and the information that is being presented. Both lines should have clearly defined starting points so that the information in the chart is not distorted, particularly the axis that represents the amounts in the graph. An axis, particularly one that shows values, may be intersected by lines. Lines that extend across the entire chart are called *grid lines*. Short lines that intersect the axis are called *tics*. These lines help the reader measure portions of the line.

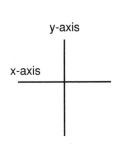

Legend. A legend is a grouping of text and symbols that helps identify the symbols used in a chart. Sometimes a legend is absolutely necessary to understand the chart. Many times a legend will be enclosed in a box, and it must always be placed in an area that does not obscure any of the chart's data.

Sometimes a chart will use a symbol only once, and that symbol can be labeled directly. In this case a legend would be redundant and should not be used. In most pie charts, for instance, the sections of the pie can be labeled directly, and a legend is not necessary.

Symbols such as bars, lines and sections of a pie chart are differentiated by *shadings* or, in computer software terms, *fills*. These fills may be screens, lines or patterns. If two such fills are used side by side, they must be different enough so that the reader can clearly identify one from the other.

The redundant legend

This chart does not need a legend because the symbols are labeled directly.

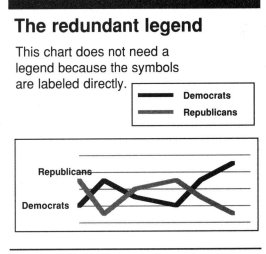

Depth and perspective. These two elements were discussed in the previous chapter in terms of what effects they have on the proportionality of a chart. Here they need be mentioned only in that they are tools that a graphic journalist can use to enhance and enliven the charts he or she creates.

Depth is the adding of sides to the elements of a chart to create an illusion that the chart is three-dimensional. Depth can also be created by shadowing; that is, the graphic journalist can put a shaded shape behind an element to make the shape appear to be off the page.

Perspective is the control the journalist exercises over the reader's view of a chart. Many computer graphing programs have sophisticated options that alter the perspective of the reader in many ways. Perspective uses depth and sometimes shadowing to create illusions and to make charts more interesting.

Depth and perspective

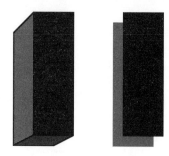

On the left, depth is created by adding a third dimension; on the right by shadowing.

Computer software programs allow journalists a wide variety of perspective options – some of which do not help the reader understand the information in the graph.

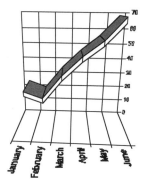

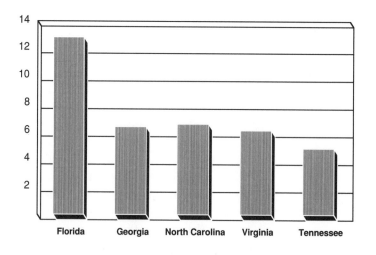

Even adding a limited amount of depth to a chart, as in this one to the right, can change the perspective and may distort the presentation of the data. Some argue that adding depth enlivens a chart and makes it more appealing to readers. The graphic journalist needs to weigh this consideration carefully against the requirement that information be accurately presented.

Most mass media publications use three types of chart-based graphics: the bar chart, which can be subdivided into the bar and column chart; the line chart; and the pie chart. (There are other types of charts for presenting numerical information such as the scattergraph, but these are not commonly found in the mass media.) Each type of chart is best used for presenting certain types of information and is inappropriate for other types of information. Journalists need to understand what charts are appropriate for what types of information.

BAR CHARTS   The bar chart is the most popular type of chart because it is easy to set up and can be used in many ways. The basic bar chart uses thick lines or rectangles that run horizontally to present its information. These rectangles represent the amounts in the information that is to be presented.

The main purpose of the bar chart is to allow readers to compare data and to show relationships with the data. A bar chart should be constructed so that the reader can see what the point of the chart is and what comparisons should be made.

Another requirement of the bar chart is that it should show some difference between or among the data. A bar chart in which the bars are essentially the same length will not tell the reader very much and will usually turn out to be a waste of space. (In some cases, the use of a bar chart can be counter-productive. It can obscure important differences in data and make them seem insignificant.)

A wide variety of bar charts are available to the graphic journalist who needs to prepare information quickly in a chart. That variety can be fitted into four major categories of bar charts: simple, grouped, subdivided and pictographs.

Simple bar charts. These charts use single bars to represent different values of one thing. Even in their simplest form, however, they can engage the reader in a wealth of information.

The simple bar chart on the next page shows the circulation figures for the five largest newspapers in the United States. Not only can the reader get an idea of what the five largest papers are and what their circulation sizes are, but the reader can also get a picture of how those sizes compare to one another. The chart shows that in 1992 the Wall Street Journal was the top circulation newspaper in the country, and that USA Today was second, but not that far behind. It also shows little difference in the circulation figures of the New York Times and the Los Angeles Times.

All of the bars in this chart have the same shading. If the graphic journalist wanted to emphasize one bar of the chart, he or she could put

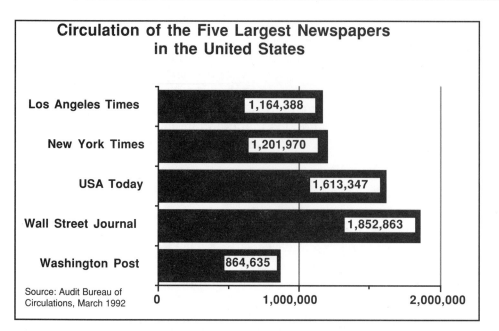

Circulation of the Five Largest Newspapers in the United States

Newspaper	Circulation
Los Angeles Times	1,164,388
New York Times	1,201,970
USA Today	1,613,347
Wall Street Journal	1,852,863
Washington Post	864,635

Source: Audit Bureau of Circulations, March 1992

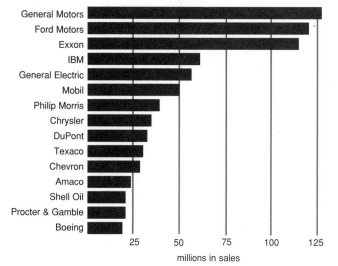

Top 15 U.S. Industrial Corporations, 1989

General Motors
Ford Motors
Exxon
IBM
General Electric
Mobil
Philip Morris
Chrysler
DuPont
Texaco
Chevron
Amaco
Shell Oil
Procter & Gamble
Boeing

25 50 75 100 125

millions in sales

The bar charts on this and the next page demonstrate the major use of this type of chart – to compare data. The viewers of these charts can study them and draw their own conclusions about the data. For instance, a reader might understand if an article said that General Motors was the largest corporation in the United States in 1989, but the chart on the left gives that reader a basis of comparison. How big is big? With the chart, the reader has some idea.

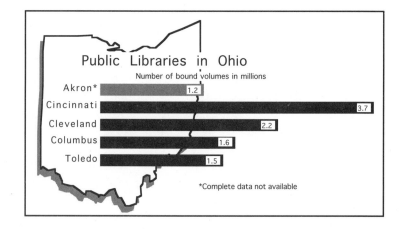

Public Libraries in Ohio

Number of bound volumes in millions

Akron*	1.2
Cincinnati	3.7
Cleveland	2.2
Columbus	1.6
Toledo	1.5

*Complete data not available

that in black and the others in gray. For instance, if this chart were to accompany an article on the increase in circulation for USA Today, the journalist might want to lighten the bars representing the other newspapers. Another use of variable shading of the bars results from incomplete data at one of the data points or data that are somehow different from other data shown in the graph.

An advantage to the simple bar chart is that it can handle a relatively large number of single pieces of data efficiently in a small space. The graph to the left on the size of the nation's largest industrial corportions shows the reader several different pieces of data and allows the reader to see thier relationship.

One of the best features of the simple bar chart is that it can be set up and manipulated with relative ease. This simple chart took less than 10 minutes to construct with a computer program, and enhancing it would not take a great deal of time.

Grouped bar charts. One of the reasons a bar chart is so popular is that it can show both amounts and relationships. The chart on this page demonstrates the bar chart's ability to show relationships, particularly when there is a large amount of data.

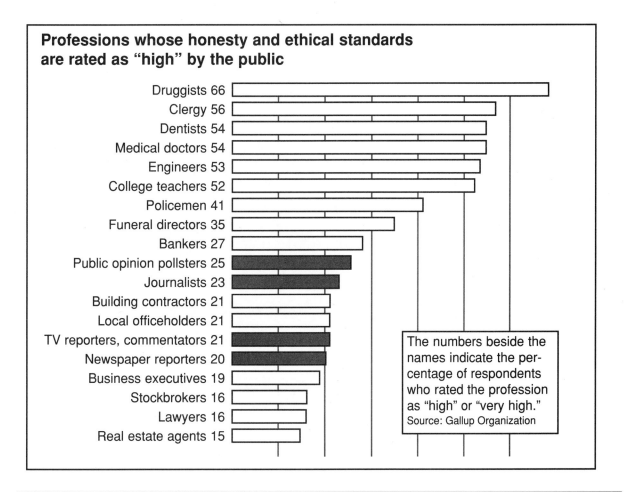

Professions whose honesty and ethical standards are rated as "high" by the public

Druggists 66
Clergy 56
Dentists 54
Medical doctors 54
Engineers 53
College teachers 52
Policemen 41
Funeral directors 35
Bankers 27
Public opinion pollsters 25
Journalists 23
Building contractors 21
Local officeholders 21
TV reporters, commentators 21
Newspaper reporters 20
Business executives 19
Stockbrokers 16
Lawyers 16
Real estate agents 15

The numbers beside the names indicate the percentage of respondents who rated the profession as "high" or "very high."
Source: Gallup Organization

From a glance at the chart below, the reader knows how these colleges compare to one another as well as something about each school. The reader can quickly see that all of the colleges have roughly the same number of students. It is obvious that Blount University admits more freshmen than the other colleges and that Shipley University has the fewest seniors. Jefferson College has the least difference between the number of freshmen and the number of seniors. What does that tell us about Jefferson College?

This chart is called a *grouped bar chart* because the bars are grouped together. Comparisons can be made within the group and between the groups. Such charts have their limits, however. The number of bars in each group here is four, and that is probably as many as there should be. Readers would have to work a good deal to compare more than four bars, and that might defeat the purpose of the chart.

Subdivided bar charts. Another type of bar chart is the subdivid-

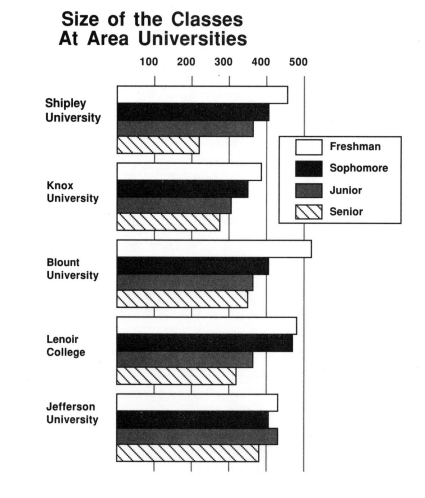

Size of the Classes
At Area Universities

ed bar graph. A single subdivided bar shows how something is divided, and the values can be expressed in absolute numbers or percentages. In the example below, a semester's grade distribution for a college is expressed in percentages. Percentages are used when the absolute number of each category is relatively unimportant.

Sometimes, however, the overall numbers are important. In the graph on "Newspaper Circulation During the Depression," each bar represents the total newspaper circulation for one year. It is then divided into sections representing morning, evening and Sunday circulation figures. This graph shows readers how these relationships changed during the years of the Depression. For instance, between 1935 and 1937, the morning circulation figures dropped, while the overall circulation for newspapers rose. Looking at the entire period, we can see that circulation dropped during the middle years but rose toward the end of the Depression. Sunday circulation also grew slightly during that period.

Grade Distribution for Fall Term

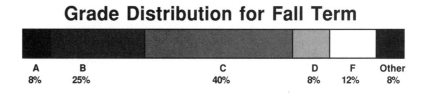

A	B	C	D	F	Other
8%	25%	40%	8%	12%	8%

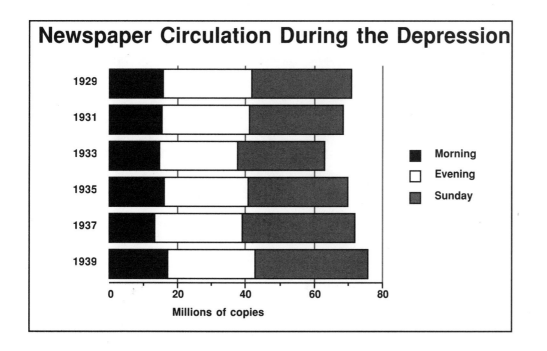

Pictographs. Rather than using bars to represent the amounts of an item, pictographs use symbols to represent the item. A pictograph is an old-fashioned form of a bar chart, but it is still popular in many publications today. Used in moderation, the pictograph offers some welcome variety to the standard rectangles of the bar chart.

While pictographs are not difficult to construct, they do require some thought, and graphic journalists should observe some of the conventions that have been developed for them. For instance, it is best to have only one symbol that is used for values in a pictograph. The symbol can be varied as needed in the graph, but the variations should not be numerous.

Symbols should be clear and self-explanatory. A casual reader should have no doubt what the symbol represents. Generally, symbols should be representations without much detail. They should represent a value that is consistent throughout the graph, and they should be constructed so they can be cut off to represent a portion of that value.

Pictographs such as the one below have largely gone out of fashion with many graphic journalists. They are seen as somewhat juvenile for many of the more sophisticated audiences. Still, they have their uses, and journalists should be familiar with the ways in which they can be constructed.

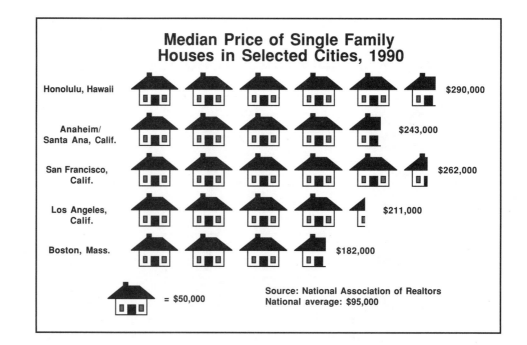

Median Price of Single Family Houses in Selected Cities, 1990

Honolulu, Hawaii — $290,000

Anaheim/Santa Ana, Calif. — $243,000

San Francisco, Calif. — $262,000

Los Angeles, Calif. — $211,000

Boston, Mass. — $182,000

= $50,000

Source: National Association of Realtors
National average: $95,000

COLUMN CHARTS

The column chart refers to bar charts in which the bars run vertically. Many people think of column charts only as bar charts whose bars are vertical rather than horizontal. The two types of charts have many similarities, but the column chart is commonly used in some instances where the bar chart would not be appropriate. Column charts are more commonly used when time is an element in the data or the relationship. As with bar charts, there are many variations and uses of column charts. We will confine our discussion to four of the most common: simple, grouped, stacked and range.

Simple column chart. These charts usually depict values of one category over a period of time. Like simple bar charts, this type of informational graphic is popular and often used because it is easy to create and easy to understand for the reader.

The simple column chart can be enhanced in a number of ways with depth and perspective and by changing the shadings of the columns. At this point, however, several questions might arise about the formation of the charts. It is difficult for the readers to determine exact amounts from looking at the columns, so should numbers representing the exact amounts be included? The answer lies in how precise the graphic journalist wants to be. The point of the graph may be to show an overall trend, rather than precise data. If that is the case, the numbers may not be necessary.

A more serious problem can lie with the data themselves. Often a journalist will have data for irregular intervals, such as with the chart on the next page. The interval between the first three columns is in 10-year

U.S. Infant Mortality Rate

A clean, simple column chart allows the reader to quickly compare the data presented in the chart. This chart presents the reader with a minimum number of lines and no distractions from the data.

Time intervals

The problem of showing time intervals in column graphs comes when the data themselves have irregular time intervals. Still, the information may be important for the reader, and the graphic journalist needs to learn to deal with this difficulty. The first graph below is not the way to deal with it. The graph shows the time between all points to be equal when it is not. The second graph separates and groups the last four data points, indicating an irrgular time interval. Is there another means to handle this problem?

U.S. Infant Mortality Rate

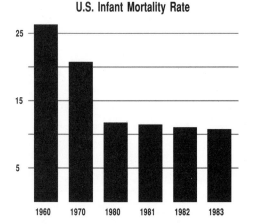

U.S. Infant Mortality Rate

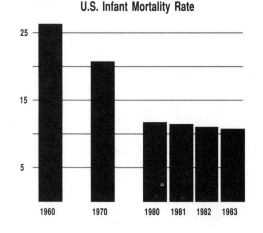

increments, but there is only a year's difference in the next four spaces. The problem with this chart is that it gives the wrong impression about the trend that is being presented. The best that a graphic journalist can do is to present data at consistent intervals. Barring that, the journalist should make some effort to visually signal to the reader that the intervals are irregular. In the second graph, the journalist has increased the space between the first three columns and connected the columns that represent a single year's differences.

Grouped column chart. In this type of chart, columns are grouped together representing different amounts of items within the same time period. Like their counterparts among the bar charts, a grouped column chart is an excellent means for making comparisons both in the time period and across time periods.

Two necessary elements for making this type of chart work are different shadings or colors and a legend that identifies those shadings or colors.

The example on the next page shows how data-rich and easy to interpret the grouped bar chart can be. We have taken our data on infant mortality rates (see the chart on the previous page) and have added the dimension of race. Now the picture that we get of infant mortality rates is quite different from the one we originally had.

Stacked column chart. The stacked column chart, like the subdivided bar chart, divides a rectangle or column representing an item into proportional parts. These stacked columns may be used one at a time or in a series to compare the divisions of several items. The columns may also show absolute values or percentages

Range or floating bar chart. This type of chart is particularly useful in showing sets of information that fluctuate and in allowing viewers to compare those sets. They show maximum and minimum values for each item or time period represented.

These charts are often used to show how temperatures fluctuate or how the price of a single

The stacked column graph below shows that all of the data in each category adds up to the same amount – in this case, 100 percent. A stacked column graph shows how the parts of a whole are divided up, much like a pie chart, which is discussed later in this chapter.

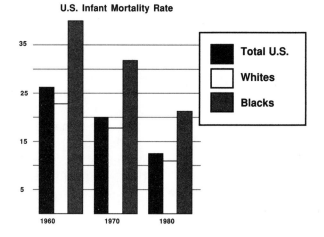

U.S. Infant Mortality Rate

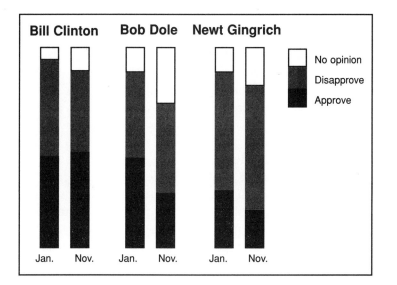

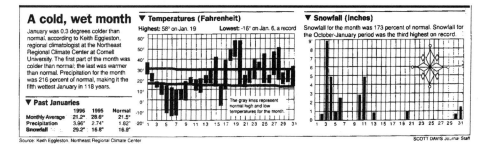

Scott Davis, Ithaca Journal

stock may go up or down in a short period of time. Any category that fluctuates within a specific time period may require a range chart.

LINE CHARTS

Whereas the column chart *may* show change over time, the line chart *must* show change over time. It can also show a change in relationships over time. In some instances, it is preferable to the bar chart because it is cleaner and easier to decipher. Line charts go by a variety of names, such as fever lines, slope charts and curve charts.

The line chart uses a line or set of lines to represent amounts and the frame of the graph represents time. One of the standard conventions of the line chart is that the x-axis represents the time element and the y-axis represents the amounts or quantities being represented.

The line chart is very flexible and widely used because of its ease in interpretation. The central idea of the line chart is the shape or direction of the lines in the chart, not the individual plotting points on the line. A reader should be able to discern the shape of the line quickly upon looking at the chart. The individual plotting points on the line should be placed as accurately as possible, but the chart is not built to highlight these points.

A number of variations of line charts exist. We will discuss four: simple line charts, multiple line charts, area or surface charts and band charts.

Simple line chart. The simple line chart is probably the most efficient chart that we have discussed in this chapter. It is very easy to set up for the graphic journalist, and it takes little time to interpret on the part of the reader. In creating the simple line graph, the journalist must make a number of style decisions, such as what shade or style to put the line in and whether or not to include plotting points, and if so, what symbols to use for these points.

The journalist may also have to contend with more serious problems in a simple line graph. One is what to do with spikes. Spikes are abberations in the data that are likely to throw the chart out of kilter. Sometimes the spike can be broken so that the shape of the chart is not damaged completely. When this occurs, the spike should be labeled so that the reader knows how to interpret the information in the graph.

A more serious problem that the graphic journalist might encounter in developing a simple line chart is the one of proportion. Lines in a line chart can be made to look either steep or gently sloping depending on the space that is allowed for the width and depth of the chart. Differences that are shown by the line can be either dramatic or smoothed out because of the proportions that the graphic journalist chooses.

The proportions of a line chart depend on the space that is available in the publication and the judgment of the graphic journalist who is creating it. There is no standard formula or guideline for determining the proper proportions of a chart. A reader should be able to see clearly the labels along both axes of the grid, and those labels should be placed horizontally rather than at a slant or vertically.

U.S. Consumption of Coal, 1978-1989
(quadrillion BTUs)

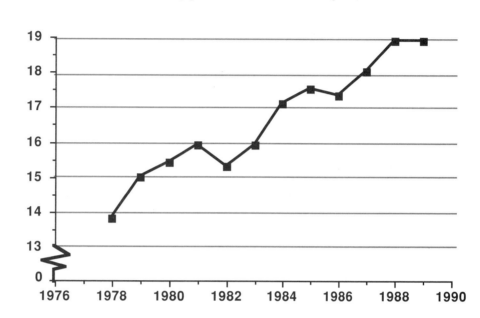

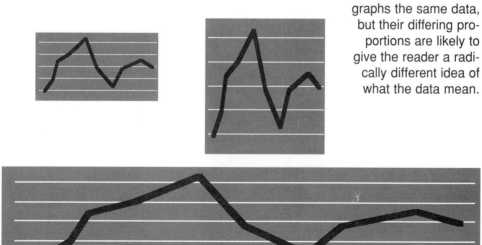

Each of these charts graphs the same data, but their differing proportions are likely to give the reader a radically different idea of what the data mean.

Multiple line chart. Line charts can use more than one line to show not only how one item has changed, but the relationship of changes of several items. These are called multiple line charts. The danger with multiple line charts is that too many lines can be confusing to the reader. While there is no rule on how many lines should be used, a chart that has more than three or four lines should be avoided. Generally, lines should be done in different styles or shadings so that the reader can distinguish between them.

Multiple line graphs are an excellent means of comparing the trends of two or more items over a given time period. They can indicate if these trends are directly or inversely related to each other.

Area or surface chart. This type of chart is good for showing how the division of something changes over time. The totals within an area may fluctuate, and the overall totals may also fluctuate. Different shadings for the areas help the reader to see how they have changed. The graph on the next page shows newspaper circulation changes during the years of the Depression – the same data that were used for the subdivided bar graph on page 45.

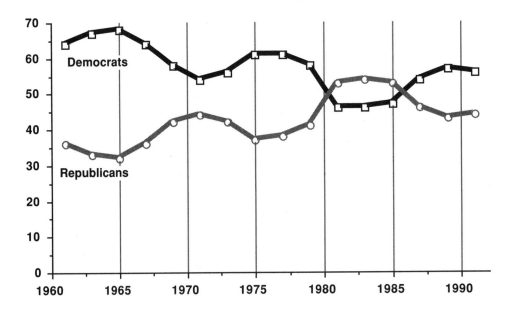

Number of Democrats & Republicans in the U.S. Senate, 1961-1991

Newspaper Circulation During the Depression

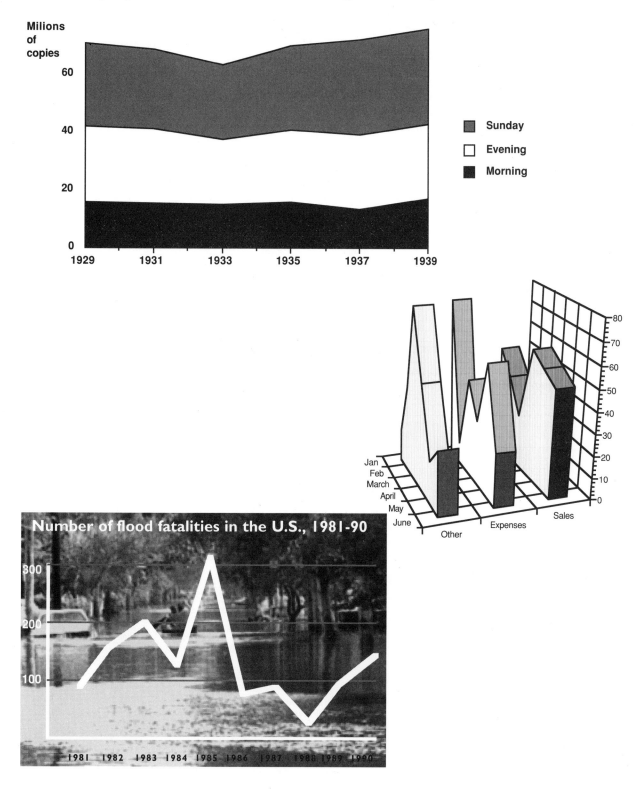

Milions of copies

Sunday
Evening
Morning

Number of flood fatalities in the U.S., 1981-90

Band chart. A band chart, also called a silhouette chart, takes elements of the multiple line graph and the area chart and puts them together for a special purpose – to emphasize the difference between two lines. The major point of the band chart is not the lines themselves or their direction but the depth of the differences that are represented. The only area shaded in this chart is the space between the two lines.

An intersecting band chart is one in which the lines intersect at one or two points. The area in a band after the intersection will be shaded differently from that before the intersection.

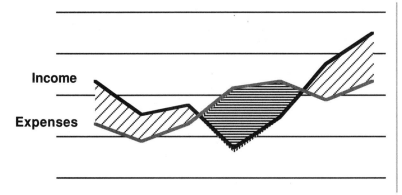

This typeical band or ribbon chart (above) shows how useful this type of chart can be.

The chart below takes a complex set of numbers and uses them to draw a clear picture for the reader. The line traces the difference between those identifying themselves as Deomcrats and as Republicans in aseries of public opinion surveys in a Southern state over a decade and a half. A reader can quickly see which party held an advantage and when.

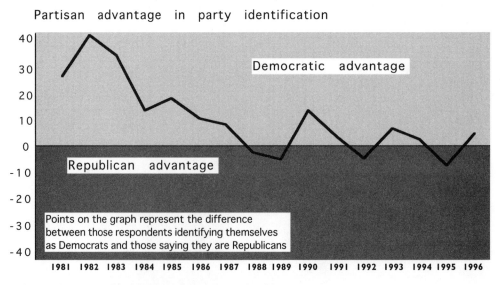

Partisan advantage in party identification

Democratic advantage

Republican advantage

Points on the graph represent the difference between those respondents identifying themselves as Democrats and those saying they are Republicans

Source: Capstone Poll and Southern Opinion Research public opinion surveys

Sidebar

THE TYRANNY OF THE ALPHABET

Jack Smith

For an informational graphic to be successful, the information it conveys must in some way be significant.

"No matter how sharp or attractive a graphic might look, if the reader doesn't immediately know why the data is important, the graphic serves no purpose," said Dan Proctor, graphics director at *The Knoxville (Tenn.) News-Sentinel*.

Too often, Proctor said, graphics journalists present information in formats that fail to illustrate the data's significance.

The simple box graphic on this page clearly illustrates Proctor's point. The graphic, which was simulated from a graphic found in a large daily newspaper, lists the results from a primary election.

Instead of listing the election totals in descending order (the candidate with the most votes first, the candidate with the least votes last), the graphic lists the candidates' results alphabetically.

"If the names at the top and bottom of a list dealing with numbers are not significant, then the graphic makes no sense," Proctor said.

While such lists of information often come to the graphics department in alphabetical order, such a format simply defies reason and fails to demonstrate to the reader anything significant.

"You must ask yourself the following question," Proctor said. "What am I trying to tell the reader is important about this graphic? It certainly is not how things are spelled."

Alphabetized lists should only be used when a list of data is exceptionally long, or when it is not necessary to make comparisons among the data, Proctor added.

Results of the 1996 Iowa GOP caucuses
(in alphabetical order)

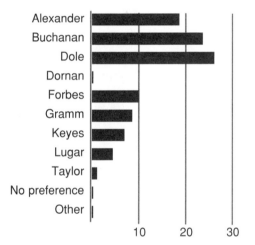

Results of the 1996 Iowa GOP caucuses
(in order of finish)

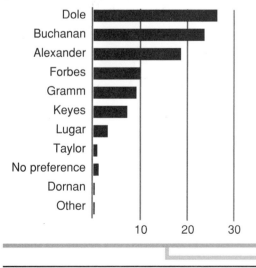

PIE CHARTS   The pie or circle chart is another popular means of showing data, but its use is specialized. A pie chart should show how an entity or item is divided, and the divisions are most commonly expressed in percentages that add up to 100 percent. Figures may also be used to identify the parts of a pie chart, but it is important that the creator of a pie chart keep the concept of percentages in mind.

Despite the strict limits of the kind of data that can be shown in a pie chart, this type of chart can be used in a variety of ways. A pie chart can show only one set of data at a time, but several pie charts can be used together to help compare sets of data, as in the set on the next page that depicts the racial breakdown of populations in three major cities. A pie chart should be clearly labeled in order to be understandable.

A number of conventions governs the construction of a pie chart:

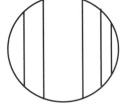

•   The circle is divided by lines that extend from the center out toward the edge. The circle is not divided by lines that simply cut across the circle itself without going through the center. (See the illustration at the left.)

•   The first "cut" of the pie is made from the center of the circle to the top, or the 12 o'clock position.

•   The pie is then divided clockwise from the largest to the smallest sections. This convention is more of a guideline than a rule. A graphic journalist may choose to divide a pie differently if the pie will look better or be more understandable. For example, it may be that certain parts of the pie should be grouped together rather than have the pieces

Elements of a pie chart

This pie chart demonstrates many of the standard conventions of pie charts

Labels are inside the slices of the pie when there is room.

The slices of the pie emanate from the center.

The pie is drawn clockwise beginning with the largest piece from the 12 o'clock position.

Whites 42%

Blacks 35%

Where your education dollar goes

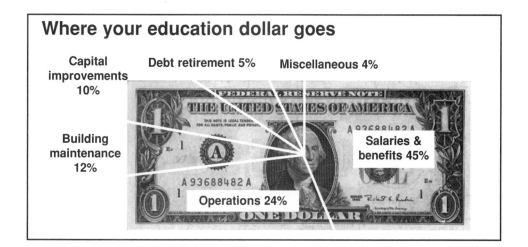

Capital improvements 10%

Debt retirement 5%

Miscellaneous 4%

Building maintenance 12%

Salaries & benefits 45%

Operations 24%

Ethnic Populations in the Three Largest Cities in the U.S.

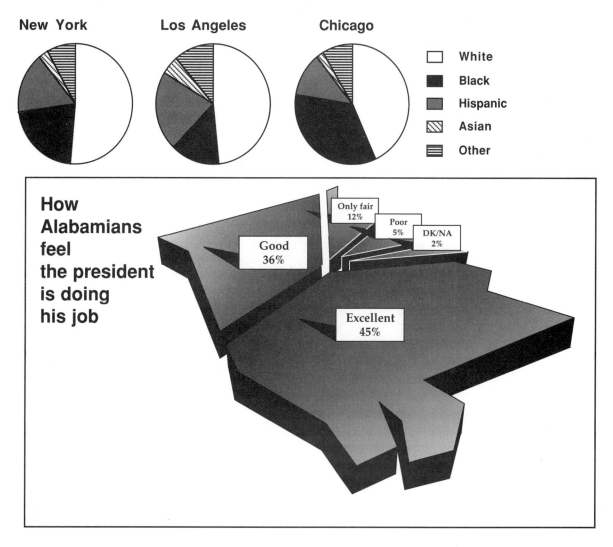

New York

Los Angeles

Chicago

- ☐ White
- ■ Black
- ▨ Hispanic
- ▨ Asian
- ▤ Other

How Alabamians feel the president is doing his job

Only fair 12%

Poor 5%

DK/NA 2%

Good 36%

Excellent 45%

arranged from largest to smallest. It is important that when two or more pies are used to compare two sets of data, they should be divided and shaded or colored in a similar manner so that they can be easily compared.

•   Most designers follow the eight-piece rule: a pie should not be divided into more than eight pieces. It is also difficult to see a piece that represents less than two percent.

A pie chart whose segments have been separated is called an exploded pie chart. This type of chart makes the segments that have been separated more distinguishable. If the creator of the chart wants to emphasize a certain part of it, this is a good way to do it.

Of all of the graphic forms discussed in this chapter, the pie chart seems to be the least vulnerable to distortion when depth is added to the graphic. Most pie charts will have some quality of depth, but the journalist still needs to be aware that this characteristic could distract a reader from the central idea or piece of information that the chart is attempting to convey.

Graphic journalists have found unusual ways to use the pie chart form. Taking shapes that are not circles and dividing them up as pie charts is something readers will occasionally see. This practice is frowned upon by informational graphic purists who believe that the conventions of charts should be strictly observed. Nevertheless, the technique can be

Chapter review and highlights

Characteristics of chart-based graphics
• Simplicity
• Consistency
• Headlines and labels
• Attribution
• Use of color

Depth and perspective
Check the information about these items in this chapter and in chapter 2.

Types of charts
Bar chart: uses horizontal bars to represent numerical data.
Column chart: use vertical bars to represent information
Line chart: represents change or over
Pie chart: represents parts of a whole

Questions
What type of chart would you use to represent the way a school budget is divided?
What type of chart would you use to show the differences in gas mileage for various models of cars?
How would you show information about how the number of acres used for farmland had changed since 1980?
What rule should be followed when using time intervals in a chart.

Coming up:
Chapter 4: Maps and the different uses that maps have.
Chapter 5: Charts without numbers; what types of charts are useful when numerical information is not involved.

artful and attention-getting, but care must be taken that the data are not distorted.

Despite their popularity, pie charts are very limited in their usefulness in presenting data. They can represent only the divisions of one item at one particular time. It is difficult for a reader to estimate percentages on a pie chart by looking at the chart itself. And even when they are relatively simply constructed, several pie charts together are not easy for the casual reader to compare.

CONCLUSION

Chart-based graphics offer the journalist useful forms in which to present numerical data. In general, they are not difficult to construct, particularly if the journalist has the proper hardware and software to create them. Their conventions of use are relatively simple to understand and adhere to.

For the journalist, the difficulty with these charts lies in the information that they are constructed to convey. That information must be accurate, it must be complete, and it must be in the proper context. The chart selected for presenting the information must be appropriate for the data. The graphic journalist has the responsibility of understanding the uses and limitations of these graphic forms.

FURTHER READING

Howard Finberg, "It was 20 years ago today, Sgt. Pepper taught the band to play," *Design*, Apr/May /June, 1994, p. 17.

Howard Finburg and Bruce Itule, *Visual Editing*, Belmont, Calif.: Wadsworth, 1990.

Nigel Holmes, *Designer's Guide to Creating Charts and Diagrams*, New York: Watson-Guptill, 1991.

Nancy I. Z. Reese, ". . . and the band plays on," *Design*, Apr/May /June, 1994, p. 17.

4

Maps

arely does a week pass at Time magazine, writes graphics director Nigel Holmes, that does not include a debate among the editors about whether or not they should use a map in the upcoming issue. "Do the readers know where Armenia is? Have they forgotten last week's map? Do they need a map *every* week of a continuing news story?" Such debates occur regularly at many of the nation's publications. At the New York Times, the pro-mapites seem to win a lot. In one recent weekday issue of the national edition, the Times included 11 different maps.*

The map is one of the most useful and used charts available to the graphic journalist. Maps have always been popular graphic devices among journalists. During the early history of graphic journalism in this country, especially during the Civil War, the map was an indispensible feature of what a publication had to tell its readers. The map has never really been out of favor with editors. Most newspapers have used weather maps for many years. The graphics revolution of the 1980s, however, saw the map used in new forms and functions. Graphics editors can buy disks full of maps that they can access and enhance on their own computers.

* December 30, 1993. The next day the Times had 9 maps, and on New Year's Day 1994, a Saturday, the paper published 6 maps in its national edition.

Software programs enable skilled graphic journalists to create their own maps for local consumption.

But do readers want to see maps? Do they take time to read them? Given the supposed geographic illiteracy, do they understand what they are reading? The answer to all of those questions is at least a tentative – and sometimes a definite – yes. Whether they understand them completely and whether they have any sense of direction, readers grow up with maps and expect to see them in their publications. We all grow up having to figure out where things are.

Maps help set the information that a journalist has into a physical and mental context for the reader. They give the readers some mental attachment to the information. Maps help highlight the differences and varieties of the lives of people that do not live in our locales.

Creating maps is neither easy nor automatic. Few maps come straight out of a computer program and onto a publication page without some enhancements. They require skill, sensitivity, knowledge and creativity. Computers help, of course. We would not see nearly as many sophisticated and creative maps as we do today without the computer. The modern mapmaker must combine geographic and journalistic

Mercator

Mercator solved some navigation problems of the 16th century by projecting his world map onto a cylinder.

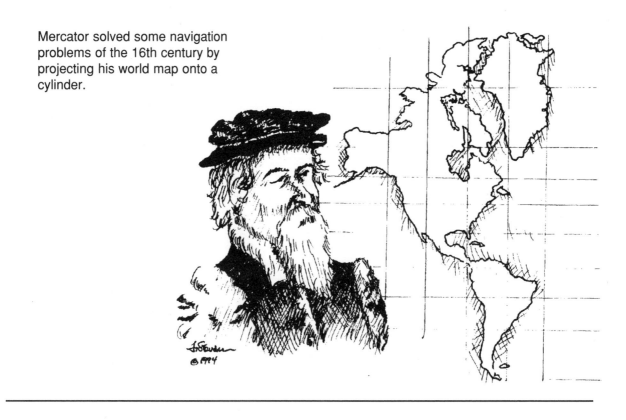

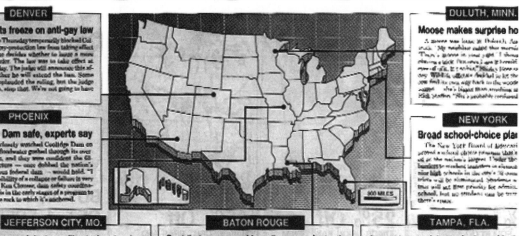

icators seek reinforcements in battle for school cont

The Jackson (Miss.) Clarion Ledger has used this map motif to unify the stories on its inside national news page. The map, the lines, and the reverse labels help the reader to identify the locations of the events in the stories.

knowledge with creativity and imagination to properly inform readers using maps. Along the way, the modern mapmaker – like counterparts throughout the centuries – is likely to have some fun.

THE MODERN MAP

The history of mapmaking is filled with intrigue and adventure – as well as fraud, greed and some of the most creative of intellectual reasoning. Mapmaking has always been an important profession, especially when we did not know the size and shape of the world and its land masses. Men and women worked for centuries to tell us where we are in relation to one another and to the universe.

The earliest maps that we know of were those of the Babylonians made some 2300 years before the birth of Christ. It's a safe bet that maps have been around ever since humans had to communicate with one another. The early days of mapmaking were marked by a lot of guesswork because there were so many gaps in our knowledge about geography. Some of the guesses that mapmakers made were reasonably accurate, and some were spectacularly wrong.

One of the giants of the history of mapmaking was Ptolemy, a

Maps became a popular graphic device in many
newspapers during the Civil War because people needed to
know where the events of the war were taking place.

second century scholar who dabbled in a variety of fields. Ptolemy was head of the great library of Alexandria, Egypt. His work with maps, and his thinking about them, left permanent marks. Ptolemy is credited with establishing the practice of orienting maps toward the north; that is, the top of a map should be the northern most point of what is being shown.

More importantly, Ptolemy taught us that maps should be drawn to scale, using "just proportions." They should be drawn proportionately to reflect the dimensions of the area they represent. To help with this, Ptolemy developed a system of north-south, east-west parallel lines that related to astronomical observations. Had the earth been flat, Ptolemy could have stopped there. But Ptolemy did not believe that the earth was flat. (Neither did the Greeks who preceded him; the flat-earth theory did not come into vogue until the Middle Ages.) That left him to struggle with the problem of depicting a round surface on a flat plane.

Thirteen centuries later Gerhardus Mercator, a Flemish geographer, offered a solution that we still see a great deal today. He devised a system of projecting a map onto a cylinder; this system, published in 1569, was designed specifically to help navigators get from one point to another. The Mercator projection, however, sacrifices realistic representations of the northern and southern parts of the globe. If you wondered why Greenland appears on many maps to be so much larger than it really is, you have Mercator to thank. His projection has been confusing school children for four centuries.

Many of the gaps in geographic knowledge have been filled today, and cartography – the practice of making maps – relies on many sophisticated instruments, including satellites. Most of the time, graphic journalists do not have to struggle with projecting rounded surfaces onto flat planes. The maps they produce do not have to take into account the curvature of the earth. Still, they do need to observe the ancient conventions of orienting the tops of maps toward the north and drawing maps to a proper scale.

Maps commonly found in the mass media fall into three categories: locator maps, data maps, and explanatory maps. As with other graphics disucssed in this book, these categories are not mutually exclusive. Some maps serve all three of these purposes; others serve two of the three. This categorization gives us some framework for disucssing the development of maps.

LOCATOR MAPS The chief purpose of most maps found in the mass media is to help the reader or viewer locate the places referred to in articles. Other purposes may emerge as maps are being developed, but that's the starting point that most graphic journalists have with maps. These types of maps are usually either flat or relief maps. Maps that do

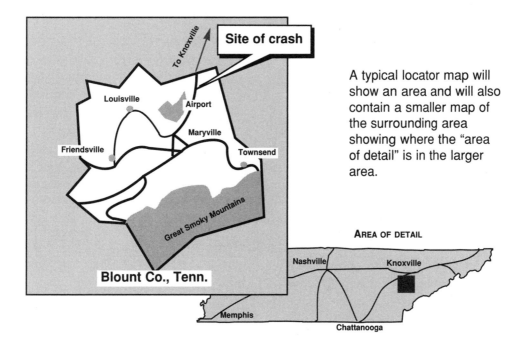

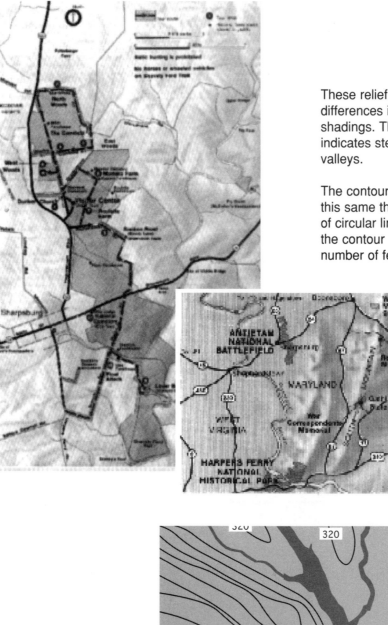

These relief maps show the differences in the topography by shadings. The darker shading indicates steeper hills and valleys.

The contour map below indicates this same thing but with a series of circular lines. The numbers on the contour map indicate the number of feet above sea level.

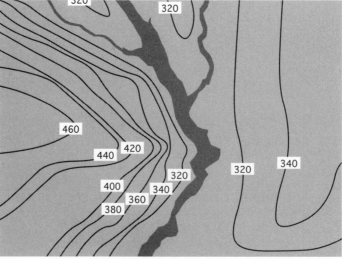

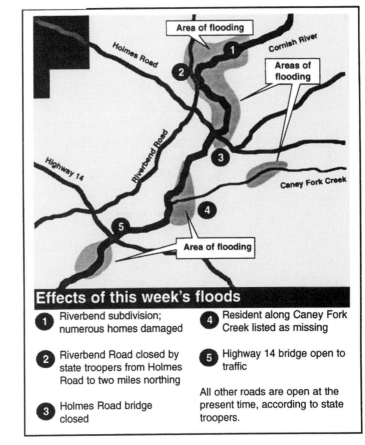

This locator map goes beyond just giving the location of an event. It relates some specific information about the effects of that event – information that the reader is likely to find useful.

not show any topographical variations – hills, valleys, and mountains – are flat. Relief maps do show some of these variations, but most of the time they do not exhibit great detail.

Most locator maps are political maps, not because they run with articles about politics, but because they show political divisions. The good locator map shows the major landmarks that will enable the reader to get an idea of where a place is. Roads, buildings, and political borders should be included. Maps of this type need to be clearly labeled. That does not mean that everything should be labeled; rather, what the reader needs to know about them should be there in type.

Areas of emphasis should have different shades or colors, and different political entities should be distinguished when appropriate. The reader should be given as many aids as possible in helping him or her understand a map. One of the conventions of locator maps is that they set bodies of water off in much darker or lighter shades than land masses. Usually, a body of water – a lake, an ocean or a river – is one of the most geographically significant elements in a map.

Most maps that cover any area at all will include some kind of a scale. The scale should be placed unobtrusively, usually in the lower part of the map. The scale need not be a major element of the map, but it should almost always be there. The graphic journalist needs to be very careful about drawing scale lines to make sure that they are accurate. The smaller the map, the more chance there is for error.

Another convention of locator maps is to include a smaller map that covers a larger area beside or within the main map. This smaller map will have a box that coincides with the area found in the main map. This box is called the "area of detail" and is usually labeled as such. Maps should also have a distinguishable outer border that indicates they are showing a finite area.

Relief maps share many of the characteristics of flat maps, but they add a third dimension that will help the reader visualize things the reader could see if her or she were actually in the location of the map. Most often, these things are mountains, valleys and rivers, but they also could include buildings and other man-made landmarks. A shaded relief map uses shadings as well as markings to distinguish various topographic formations. Relief maps take some skill and artistic ability to produce, but they are not beyond the reach of most graphic journalists. What is important about relief maps is that they be done correctly. The journalist needs more commitment to accuracy than artistic ability.

Beyond just the labels, text is often superimposed on maps to make them understandable to readers. A map – even an accurate and well-labeled map – may not make the point with the reader that the graphic journalist seeks to make. In the example on the next page, a map accompanies a story about the capture of suspects in a series of armed robberies. The map locates various cities in the area, but it is only in the thirteenth paragraph of the story that the reader can find out that these are the places where the robberies have occurred. A text block pointing to where the suspects were arrested points to an unlabeled spot on the map. To give the reader a better understanding of what has happened, the map should include a label that describes exactly where the suspects were arrested. It should also include text blocks pointing to the different locations where the armed robberies took place; these text blocks should give the dates of the robberies and some details about each of them.

Not all maps need to be of what we could consider geographic locations. The floor plans of a building can also be considered a map and can be used as such. A map could be made of the brain, a car engine, or practically any physical object. Graphic journalists who create these kinds of maps do not need to observe the convention of north orientation, but they often do need to observe the convention of scale. Just as with geographic maps, these other types of maps should have parts that are easily distinguishable for the reader and well labeled.

DATA MAPS

Maps have saved people's lives. In 1854, central London experienced an outbreak of cholera. In searching for a way to arrest the spread of the sickness, John Snow, a local physician, took a map of the area where the deaths occurred and plotted with dots the residence of everyone who had died of cholera. He also marked the location of the public water pumps in the area. His map indicated that

Sidebar

DEVELPING A MAP FILE

Jack Smith

Creating accurate locator maps for news stories can seem like a daunting task. Earnest Hart, graphics director at the Jackson (Miss.) Clarion-Ledger, said a good map file can make the difference at deadline.

"To get started with site maps, you have to have a good base map of your coverage area," Hart said. "After you have a few good base maps in your computer, you just call up a map and update it for the story."

Hart suggests starting with an atlas.

"We drew our base maps in Aldus Freehand, looking at a road atlas and maps from the state highway department," Hart said.

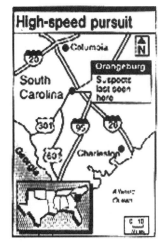

The most valuable resource, however, is the reporter covering a breaking news event.

"When reporters go out to cover a story, we always encourage them to bring back a map, especially if the story happens in an obscure town. Then we just add it to our collection."

When reporters at the Clarion-Ledger react to spot news stories, the graphics department usually follows.

"When there is a bad wreck or a complicated story, we usually go along," Hart said.

Another time-saving trick involves a simple Polaroid camera. By taking snapshots at the scene of an accident, Hart and his staff can more efficiently recreate the scene back at the office.

Instantly available snapshots also ensure accuracy, Hart said.

many of the deaths were clustered around the Broad Street water pump. Upon discovering this, he had the handle of the pump removed and thus ended the cholera that had claimed more than 500 lives in that area.

Snow used what we refer to as a data map as a life-saving device. A data map places numerical data on geographic locations in a way that will produce relevant information about the data. Data maps can aid in our understanding of the data and the areas in which it occurs. Data maps also allow readers to view large amounts of information at a single sighting in an orderly and logical way.

Three types of data maps are readily available to graphic journalists: shaded or shaded maps, dot maps and isoline maps.

Shaded maps. These maps put various geographic areas into different colors or shadings, and a legend explains what the different shadings mean. Usually, the shadings represent statistical differences but not always. For instance, a map of the United States showing what

Dr. Snow's map

This map produced by Dr. John Snow helped curb a cholera epidemic in London in 1854. By plotting cholera deaths on a street map, Dr. Snow was able to identify wells that were helping spread the disease.

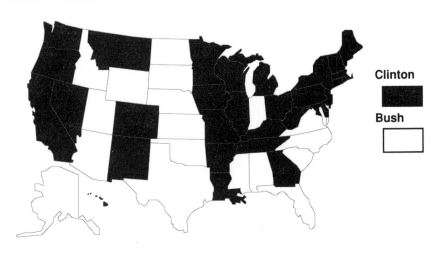

The results of the 1992 presidential election are represented on this simple data map.

Dr. Snow's data map on the opposite page used dots to locate the information. The two on this page use shading to related the information to the geographic area.

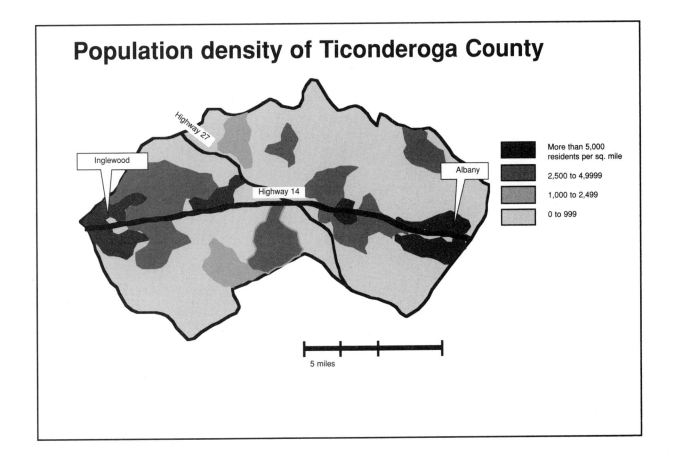

Death by . . .

A state-by-state look at methods of capital punishment in the U.S.

Electrocution – 10 states

Firing squad – 2 states

Hanging – 4 states

Lethal injection – 23 states

Gas chamber – 5 states

No death penalty – 10 states

Sources: Topeka Capital-Journal, Associated Press, NAACP Legal Defense and Education Fund and Bureau of Justice statistics

states have the death penalty and what states do not. The states that do would have the same dark fill and the states that do not would share a common light fill. One convention about these maps that is not always observed is that areas in white are not represented by any data. This convention has pretty much gone out of use because readers are not readily familiar with it.

Shaded maps are very popular and relatively easy to produce, but they present a major problem to the journalist and the reader. That problem is that the shadings do not offer any information about the variations within a shaded region. Let's say that a shaded map was drawn to show the high school dropout rates for each state and that New York had a dropout rate of 33.7 percent while New Jersey had a rate of 19.6 percent. The two states would certainly have different shadings, but we would not have any idea if the highest dropout rates for those states were concentrated in certain areas or if they were evenly distributed across both states.

This example demonstrates that using small geographic or political units helps convey more precise information in shaded maps. On the other hand, using smaller areas increases the time and effort that it takes to research and produce such a map. Given these difficulties, graphic journalists and their editors need to decide how much time and effort a shaded map is worth.

Dot maps. The dot map uses dots or some other symbol to represent the geographic distribution of something. Dr. Snow's life-saving map was a dot map. The dot map gets around the problem of shaded maps by depending not so much on political divisions as geographic locations.

Dot maps have their own difficulties, however. They are very hard and time consuming to construct. Finding data that would suit itself to the dot map is also difficult. Because dots are small, their placement on the map should coincide with the closely with the geographic location they represent, and data of this kind is not always readily available.

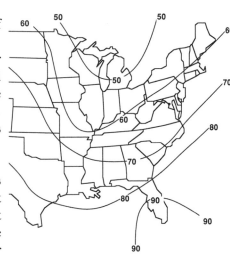

Isoline maps. Isoline maps use lines across maps to present data to the reader. The most common isoline map found in the mass media today is the weather map. These isoline maps show temperature variations and the movements of fronts and pressure systems with lines.

This typical isoline map shows the distribution of temperatures across the United States.

Speaking English

Some 22 states and many municipalities have declared English as the official language and have limited the use of other languages by the government.

When it happened

Indiana
Kentucky
Tennessee
1984
California
Georgia
1986
Arkansas
Mississippi
N. Carolina
N. Dakota Alabama
S. Carolina **1990**
1987   Montana
Arizona   New
Colorado Hampshire

Louisiana
1810

Nebraska
1920

Virginia
1950

Illinois
1969

Hawaii
1978

Florida
1988

S. Dakota
1995

1800   1850   1900   1950   2000

This data map is effectively combined with a time line to give the reader some historical perspective on the information that is presented.

A type of isoline map is the contour map. Contour maps present topographic information to the reader about hills, mountains, rivers, lakes and valleys. One type of contour map uses circular lines to indicate elevations from sea level of different parts of an area. The closer the lines are together, the steeper the slope is at that point. Another type of contour map is the color contour map in which different colors represent different elevations. Because brown is often used for the higher elevations and green for the lower elevations, people often misread these maps. They believe that the green represents vegetation and the brown lack of vegetation. Because of this misreading, graphic journalists should be careful with their use.

Contour maps are closely related to the relief maps mentioned earlier in this chapter. They both show the same things: variations in the topography of an area.

Data maps take time and effort to produce, and they should be created with great care. Data maps that are not carefully thought out can allow viewers to reach superficial or incorrect conclusions. The central questions to ask about data maps are, "Does geography make a difference to the data? If so, do those differences matter?"

EXPLANATORY MAPS Some maps do more than just show us where events took place or relate some numerical information to geographic location. They help us to understand events and places. Two types of maps are important in our considerations at this point. They are the sequence map and the facts map.

This sequence map leads the reader through an event and gives the reader a bird's eye view of the entire scene.

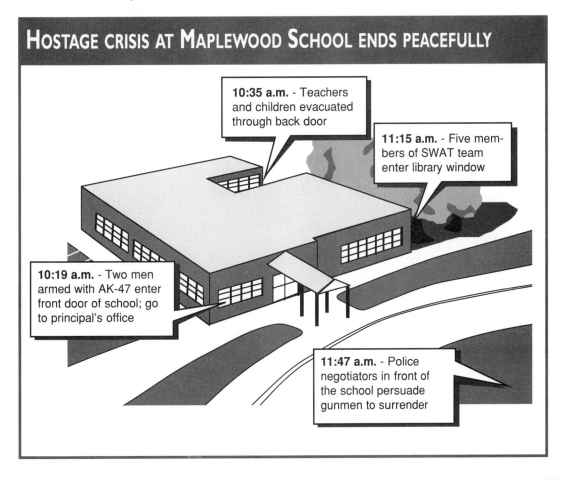

HOSTAGE CRISIS AT MAPLEWOOD SCHOOL ENDS PEACEFULLY

10:35 a.m. - Teachers and children evacuated through back door

11:15 a.m. - Five members of SWAT team enter library window

10:19 a.m. - Two men armed with AK-47 enter front door of school; go to principal's office

11:47 a.m. - Police negotiators in front of the school persuade gunmen to surrender

VICTIMS OF A DEADLY DAWN

How events unfolded

Sometime before 7 a.m.: With the house at 1046 Danby Road already engulfed in flames, Marlin Washburn, the father of six children in the house, Linda Ortega, the father's live-in girl-friend, and 3-year-old Gerrit Washburn, escape from a rear entrance. Five other children are trapped on the second floor.

7:10 a.m.: Mickey Herzing, owner of Big Al's Hilltop Quik-stop, sees the fire from his convenience store a quarter-mile away and calls the fire department. At about the same time, Leon Farley, a neighbor, tries to get into the burning house. Two more neighbors call the fire department.

7:11 a.m.: Herzing joins Farley and they both attempt to enter the house. Smoke and flames force them to retreat. A short time later, Farley holds a ladder and Herzing climbs to the second floor, but flames shoot out the lower window and again force them to pull back.

7:12 a.m.: Engine 905 from

the Ithaca Fire Department's South Hill station arrives. The worst of the blaze is under control within two minutes.

Between 7:15 and 7:20 a.m.: Firefighters extinguish the remain-ing flames and discover the bodies of five children on the second floor. Two show some vital signs and are rushed to Tompkins Community Hospital. They are pro-nounced dead a short time later.

Within the next hour: Gerrit Washburn is taken to Tompkins Community Hospital and is later released. Marlin Washburn and Ortega also are taken to TCH and admitted for observation.

Investigators believe the fire started here, in a bedroom where two adults and one child were sleeping. They escape through a backdoor.

Franklin Crawford and Scott Davis/Journal Staff

• Five brothers and sisters, ages 3 to 8, die in house fire
• Two adults, one child survive fast-moving blaze
• Cause of fire still unclear; arson ruled out

By FRANKLIN CRAWFORD
Journal Staff

It is one of the deadliest fires in Tompkins County history.

The blaze that claimed five Ithaca children's lives early Saturday morn-ing also will be remembered as one of the most emotionally devastating.

"This event is a tragedy," Ithaca Fire Department Chief Brian Wilbur said Saturday. "It's an absolute tragedy for the family, neighbors, and for all the emergency service people who did everything possible to pre-vent it."

Three people survived the blaze. Marlin Washburn, the father, Linda Ortega, his live-in girlfriend, and Ger-rit Washburn, 3, were in a first-floor bedroom when the fire erupted and they escaped through a rear door. Two other children who live in the house were away for the weekend.

Washburn is separated from the deceased children's mother, Lisa Van Zile.

Arson has been ruled out as a cause of the blaze, but fire officials and sheriff's investigators are still try-

some of whom could be heard screaming from the second floor.

"It's a really awful, helpless feel-ing," said Leon Farley, a neighbor and one of the first to arrive at the scene. "I was really trying to get in there."

Farley's comments were echoed by many of the more than 50 Ithaca fire-fighters who arrived just minutes later. After extinguishing the blaze within two minutes, the crews found the five children, three in the hallway and two huddled in the corner of a bed.

Site of fire

Journal Staff

They heard the crying, but couldn't help

This explanatory map was done with the collaboration of a reporter and a graphic journalist (Franklin Crawford and Scott Davis of the Ithaca Journal). It combines a good deal of text and a drawing to help the reader see what happened in this tragic event.

Chapter review and highlights

Early mapmaking

• **Ptolemy,** a second century scholar, established the practice of orienting maps toward the north, and he was the first to draw maps "to scale."

• **Mercator,** a 16th century Flemish geographer, helped solve the problem of depicting a round surface on a flat plane. He projected a map on a cylinder, helping navigators get from one point to another

Modern maps commonly found in the mass media:

• **Locator maps**: Usually flat or relief maps, these maps simply help the reader locate places referred to in an article. Good locator maps show roads, buildings, and political borders, and they indicate major landmarks that help the reader understand where a place is.

• **Data maps**: John Snow's 19th century map that demonstrated the cause of a cholera epidemic was a data map. These maps place numerical data on geographic locations in a way that produces relevant information about the data. There are three types of data maps: chloropleth maps, dot maps, and isoline maps.

• **Explanatory maps**: These maps do more than show the reader where events took place. They contain information that helps the journalist explain events and places.

Sequence maps actually show the reader what happened with the use of maps, photographs, and drawings of a place along with some textual explanation of the event.

Fact maps are more static than sequence maps. They are often used as backdrops to relate a good bit of information to the reader. The National Geographic Society frequently uses elaborate fact maps to relate large amounts of information about a place.

The sequence map is as close as print can come to simulating what television can sometimes do – that is, showing what happened. Sometimes television can do this, if a video camera happens to be pointed at the event. Despite their pervasiveness, however, video cameras do not capture the events that we would like to "see." For those events, we can use the sequence map.

The sequence map uses a map, photograph, or drawing of a place along with some textual explanation of an event. If the sequence of the event is not apparent, the text might include numbers or letters to help guide the reader through the event. A sequence map takes a great deal of times, effort, and skill on the part of the journalist to create. The journalist must have the relevant information in hand and must understand what he or she is trying to show the readers. If the map is drawn, either by hand or with the computer, the journalist will need to exhibit a high degree of skill with the hardware and software involved.

The idea of perspective is important in a sequence map. Often the map will include a wider area than can be included in a single photograph, and it will have an aerial or "bird's eye" view. Visualizing such scenes requires some time and thought as well as a good deal of detailed information.

The facts map is somewhat more static than a sequence map. This type of map uses a map as a backdrop in order to relate a good bit of information to the reader. It might be combined with other symbols, pictures, or drawings as the information requires. The National Geographic Society publishes superb fact maps that often take weeks or months for its journalists and catographers to produce. They can engage the readers for long periods of times, relate a mountain of information, and help the reader to visualize the information that is contained in them.

One of the most famous maps in U.S. political history is the gerrymander. When painter Gilbert Stewart saw the way the Massachusetts legislature had created a district, he drew a head, wings, and claws on it so that it resembled a salamander. An editor renamed it gerrymander after the state's governor, Elbridge Gerry.

GETTING CREATIVE

Because maps are such a standard part of our visual repertoire, you can find many examples of very creative people taking liberties with them. Shapes of states and nations become symbols rather than means of communicating geographic facts. These symbols when used throughout copy can be effective means of helping readers distinguish between different sets of information.

The shapes of geographic areas can also be used in even more creative ways. The maps may resemble geographic maps at first glance, but on closer inspection the reader finds they make quite a different point. The art of using maps to make a point goes back several centuries and is being carried on with great vigor today.

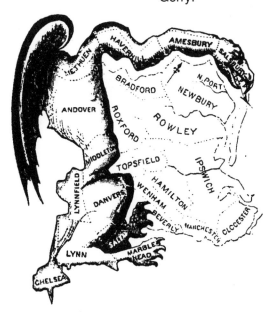

Such uses of maps are certainly legitimate. They can be fun for the graphic journalist to produce and can bring home important information and ideas to the reader.

CONCLUSION

Maps are an extremely important part of today's information mix. We live in an increasingly mobile society, and on a personal level each of us carries a set of maps in our heads. Because modern communication media have drawn the world more closely together (without necessarily peaceful results), the ideas we have of distance and location are even more important than ever. Maps help us discern who we are and where we are.

FURTHER READING

Nigel Holmes, *Pictoral Maps,* New York: Watson-Guptill Publications, 1991.

John Noble Wilford, *The Map Makers,* New York: Alfred A. Knopf, 1981.

5

Charts
without numbers

Some concepts, ideas and information cannot be easily articulated. They need a graphic form to give them life and meaning to an audience. When we think of how a college is organized, how a family tree has developed or how a jet engine works, chances are we do not try to put that into words. Instead, we form pictures in our heads, and the words come after that.

In Chapter 3 we looked at charts that presented information based on numerical data and examined some of the conventions and customs that have been developed for presenting such information. In the previous chapter, we looked at a specialized type of chart – the map – that is also based on numerical data. In this chapter we examine charts that have ideas rather than numbers at their center. While these charts may involve numerical data, such data are not at the heart of what the graphic journalist is attempting to convey.

Rather, these charts try to give viewers a picture of the relationship of the elements of information that they contain. Just as in the charts discussed in Chapter 3, the *relationship* of the parts of these charts is the crucial concept that the journalist is trying to show. In order to do this, the journalist will combine a variety of visual elements, including words, lines, boxes, and illustrations. These charts are much more dependent on words and type than charts discussed in Chapters 3 and 4. Yet the visual elements are just as important.

One important point should be made concerning the purpose of the charts presented here. Even more than the charts in Chapters 3 and 4, these charts are built to help a viewer *understand* the information and ideas being presented, not just to inform the views about them. A graphic journalist who uses these charts is trying to explain and educate, not simply present. A journalist should have this function in mind when researching and building these charts.

The three types of charts we will explore in this chapter are process, structural and time charts. Process charts are for information that is dynamic or changing in nature, and they are often used to convey the nature of this change to the viewer. Structure charts present information of a more static nature to the viewers. While what is being presented in the chart – the structure of an organization, for instance – may change, the purpose of the chart is not necessarily to show that change. Rather, it is to capture the structure of the information at a single point. Time charts have time, or history, as the central or unifying element in the information.

To talk about three types of charts implies a discreetness that is not often found in the real world. Graphic journalists often use combinations of these types of charts to convey the information and ideas that they have. We discuss three types of charts here merely as a matter of organizational convenience. The purpose of this discussion is not to enable the reader to identify and separate these types of charts. Rather, it is to help the reader to understand these means of conveying information and to be able to use them as maleable tools for his or her own purposes. A chart should serve the information it seeks to present.

PROCESS CHARTS   The process chart is the general name given to a chart that emphasizes a procedure or the way in which something happens. These charts show some movement or dynamic process. Anything that you buy that needs to be assembled probably has a process chart as part of the instructions. For our purposes, there are three types of process charts: flow charts, procedure or progress charts, and cosmographs.

Flow charts. A flow chart shows some movement through some structure or procedure. The steps in this movement can present alternatives. One flow chart that many high school civics students are familiar with is the one that shows how a piece of legislation can become law. At several points along the way, the bill can be changed, killed or re-routed. These charts use a linear flow, often represented by a single line or arrow.

A flow chart can also be a graphic representation of the entire process. In this representation, numerous arrows or lines can demon-

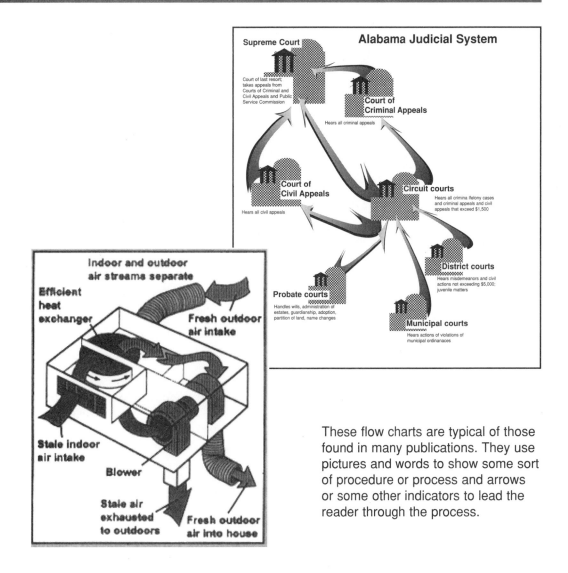

Alabama Judicial System

Supreme Court

Court of last resort; takes appeals from Courts of Criminal and Civil Appeals and Public Service Commission

Court of Criminal Appeals

Hears all criminal appeals

Court of Civil Appeals

Hears all civil appeals

Circuit courts

Hears all crimina lfelony cases and criminal appeals and civil appeals that exceed $1,500

District courts

Hears misdemeanors and civil actions not exceeding $5,000; juvenile matters

Probate courts

Handles wills, administration of estates, guardianship, adoption, partition of land, name changes

Municipal courts

Hears actions of violations of municipal ordinanaces

Indoor and outdoor air streams separate

Efficient heat exchanger

Fresh outdoor air intake

Stale indoor air intake

Blower

Stale air exhausted to outdoors

Fresh outdoor air into house

These flow charts are typical of those found in many publications. They use pictures and words to show some sort of procedure or process and arrows or some other indicators to lead the reader through the process.

strate how something flows through the process and the different routes that it can take. One such case might be a floor plan of an office that shows how work is routed around the office and what can happen to different types of work at different points. This type of representation uses many of the principles of maps discussed in the previous chapter.

A procedure or progress chart does many of the same things as a flow chart. The major difference between a procedure and a flow chart is that what is being represented has few or no alternatives in the procedure. For instance, a chart could be set up on how a shirt is made. This chart would follow the progress of the manufacture of the shirt, but there would be no alternatives along the way. Every time a shirt is made, the same steps are followed; there is no branching at any point. The distinction between a flow and a procedure chart is a fine one, and in most instances it does not make a great deal of difference.

What is quite different, however, is the cosmograph. A cosmograph

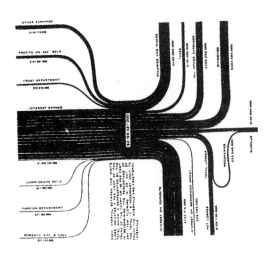

A cosmograph is structurally distinctive because, just as a chart-based graphic, it uses bars to represent its elements. This type of graph is rarely found in the mass media today.

is the one chart in this chapter that is most likely to be based on numerical data. A cosmograph has three parts: input into a processing unit, the processing unit itself, and output from the processing unit. The cosmograph is most often used with accounting. It will chart the amount and sources of income into an organization and the amount and types of expenditures the organization makes.

A cosmograph uses lines representing amounts that flow into some symbol for the processing unit. At the other end of the symbol, the lines flow out, again representing amounts of output. There may be other symbols on a cosmograph representing the sources of the input and the destination of the output. Cosmographs are not used a great deal in the mass media, but they are found occasionally, and they do have a function that graphic journalists may find very useful.

STRUCTURE CHARTS

Rather than showing a dynamic or changing process, some charts take a snapshot of some idea or set of facts as it exists at a particular moment. These are structure charts. Their purpose is not to show change but to show stability. Four type of structure charts will be discussed here: organization charts, tree charts, pictorial charts and word charts.

Organization charts. The organization chart is one of the most common charts that we are likely to encounter. It shows the hierarchical relationships within an organization at a given time. The key to an organizational chart's effectiveness is its simplicity. In a relatively short amount of time, a viewer can get a good idea of how an organization is structured and of the relationships among the positions within the organization. The viewer can also learn something about how the organization works.

Organization charts, because they emphasize hierarchy and because they do not demonstrate subtleties within the unit, are sometimes the objects of controversy. They may confer authority or hierarchy that does not exist in reality, and they do not demonstrate how easily some relationships within the organization can change. Consequently, some units try to avoid putting their structures into an organizational chart, preferring to allow centers of authority and other relationships to develop and dissolve with the people and tasks within the unit. A law firm with a number of partners and associates would assign various duties in the operation of the firm to various people. The importance of those duties and the status of the people assigned to them might not match up per-

When President Franklin Roosevelt first proposed the Civilian Conservation Corps, he drew this organizational chart for his advisers. When Congress authorized the corps, its organization was remarkably like what Roosevelt had originally envisioned.

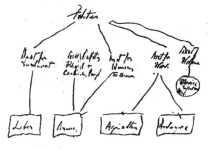

fectly, and for the sake of the smooth day-to-day operation of the firm, an organization chart should be avoided.

Because organization charts are so common, a number of graphic conventions have developed about their use. Among these conventions are the following:

• Their general shape is that of a pyramid with the highest levels of authority at the top. The higher on the chart a position is, the more authority that position has. Consequently, there are fewer positions at the top than at the bottom of the chart.

• The major graphic elements in an organization chart are boxes that surround the name of positions and/or people and lines that connect the boxes to show relationships. A solid line shows a direct, authoritative relationship; a dotted line shows shows some relationship between two

This organizational chart shows the way that many newspapers are organized. Almost any unit where there are lines of authority can be pictured in this way.

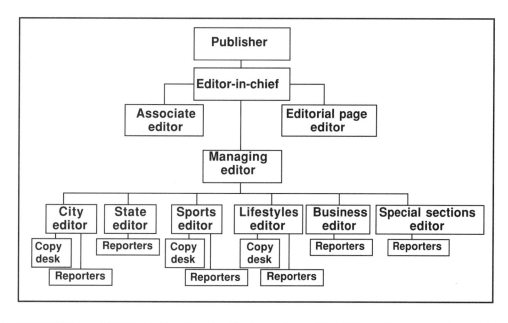

boxes, but that relationship may not be direct or authoritative. At the very least, the two positions are required to communicate in some way and under some circumstances.

• Charts should be drawn so that the lines do not cross. If solid lines cross, that implies some connection between the positions or the lines of authority. Sometimes it is impossible to draw the chart without having lines cross that have no connection with one another. In this case, a semicircle in the line at the intersection indicates they are not connected.

• In some charts, type size is smaller at the bottom of the chart than at the top. This is another indication of the power and authority of those at the top.

• Some organization charts use shadings or colors to indicate how some areas of the unit are separated from others. These differentiations can be important to the viewer in understanding how the unit is structured and how its parts work together.

Tree charts. The family tree is a common concept and expression in our society. Its meaning is fairly clear to all of us – tracing the history of our ancestors. The concept is based on a visual chart that resembles the branches of a tree.

The tree chart is the first cousin to the organization chart, but there are important differences. The main purpose of the tree chart is to show

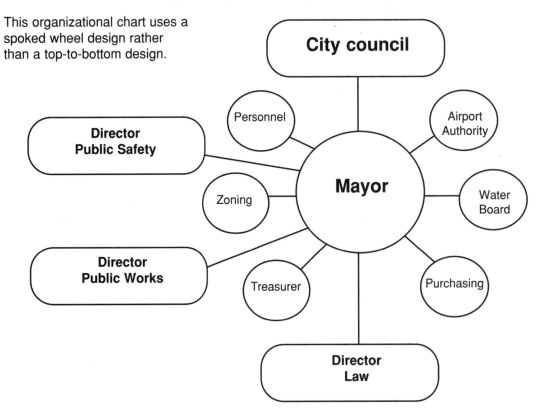

This organizational chart uses a spoked wheel design rather than a top-to-bottom design.

Pictorial chart

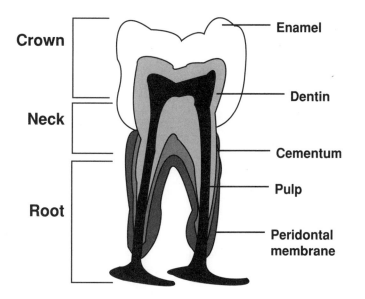

Crown

Neck

Root

Enamel

Dentin

Cementum

Pulp

Peridontal membrane

This pictorial chart uses a typical "cut-away" view of an object to give the viewers an idea of what it looks like on the inside and how its different parts work.

relationships, not lines of power or authority. It may also have the purpose of showing how something has developed up to the moment that it has been visualized.

Graphically, the tree chart has some important differences from the organization chart. As a real tree, it starts from the bottom up. The source of the unit is at the bottom rather than the top. The tree chart is less structured and rigid than an organization chart. A tree chart is more adaptive to the structure of the unit that is being pictured. It also emphasizes the graphic elements more than an organization chart.

A specialized type of tree chart is the decision tree. This chart begins at the top with a problem and a set of options or solutions. Each of the options branches off into a series of additional options, solutions or problems. Sometimes such a solution or option may be the same for two problems in two different branches of the tree. What is demonstrated is that someone can come to a solution through different routes. Creating a decision tree take a great deal of understanding, information and skill on the part of the graphic journalist.

Pictorial charts. One of the most common structure charts found in newspapers, magazines and books is the pictorial chart. This chart presents a drawing or picture of an object and identifies its parts with labels. Although it may describe the process or function of an object with words, the graphic does not show it.

This type of chart relies heavily on a graphic representation of the object. That representation must be unambiguous, and the parts of the

Word charts

Periodic Table of the Elements

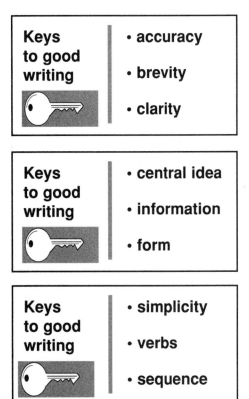

Keys to good writing	• accuracy
	• brevity
	• clarity

Keys to good writing	• central idea
	• information
	• form

Keys to good writing	• simplicity
	• verbs
	• sequence

Word charts come in many forms and serve a wide variety of purposes. Above is the periodic table of elements, a standard chart in most chemistry classrooms. This chart forms the basis for much of our knowledge about chemistry.

Word charts, such as those to the left, are typically used in slide presentations.

object must be differentiated clearly. The relationship between the parts of the object is implied by their proximity but is not demonstrated by the graphic itself.

One of the techniques often used in this type of chart is the cutaway. A cutaway drawing shows an object as if it has sliced in the center and allows us to look at the inside of an object – something that in many cases we are not likely to see. The cutaway is an excellent way of adding to our understanding of the internal elements of an object.

Word charts. Sometimes the best way to represent ideas orinformation is with words. Symbols, pictures, drawings and other graphics are not central to understanding the information. A word chart uses relatively few words to indicate a much larger set of information. Word charts are most often used in oral presentations, but they also have some usefulness in print.

Word charts generally follow the concept of an outline. A subject is broken into topics and subtopics. The listings of topics and subtopics should be typographically consistent in order to allow the viewer to make the correct conclusions about their relationships and connections. For instance, all topics should be in the same typeface and typesize; subtopics should be in a consistent but small typesize and possibly a different typeface. Sub-subtopics should be in an even smaller typesize.

Because word charts primarily use type, they are thought of as not as interesting as other kinds of charts. The use of symbols, shades and colors can keep them from being so sterile. Still, the creator of a word chart must not let the symbols distract or get in the way of understanding the material that is presented.

The most effective word charts have a unifying theme and try to make a specific point rather than simply presenting information about a topic. They should allow the viewer to make comparisons within the subject matter.

TIME CHARTS The history of a situation or subject helps place it in a context and often makes it more understandable for a reader. Time charts, sometimes called time lines, are important graphic devices for achieving this understanding.

The time chart uses some division of time as the basis for presenting the history of a subject. The central graphic element is a line that denotes a time period. The line can run vertically or horizontally depending on the needs of the graphic journalist. The following are a few of the graphic conventions that have developed in constructing time lines:

•   The line itself is divided into equal parts according to the unit of time that is being represented. Each day, year or century takes up the same portion of the line.

•   Important dates or time periods are noted by short lines that

Time lines

Time lines appear in a wide variety of forms and can use many artistic elements and techniques. Time lines carry a great deal of information, and the graphic journalist needs to be sure that the information is accurately presented.

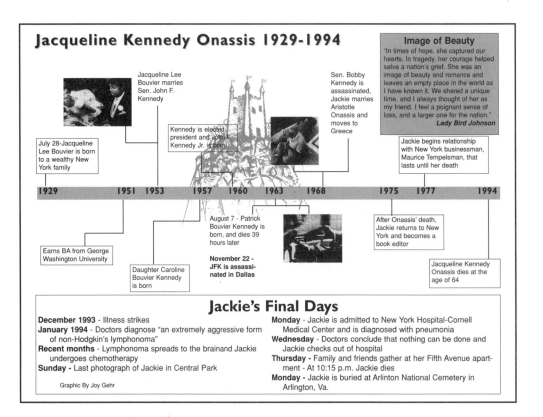

Jacqueline Kennedy Onassis 1929-1994

Jacqueline Lee Bouvier marries Sen. John F. Kennedy

July 28-Jacqueline Lee Bouvier is born to a wealthy New York family

Kennedy is elected president and John F. Kennedy Jr. is born

Sen. Bobby Kennedy is assassinated, Jackie marries Aristotle Onassis and moves to Greece

Image of Beauty
"In times of hope, she captured our hearts. In tragedy, her courage helped salve a nation's grief. She was an image of beauty and romance and leaves an empty place in the world as I have known it. We shared a unique time, and I always thought of her as my friend. I feel a poignant sense of loss, and a larger one for the nation."
Lady Bird Johnson

Jackie begins relationship with New York businessman, Maurice Tempelsman, that lasts until her death

| 1929 | 1951 1953 | 1957 1960 1963 1968 | 1975 1977 | 1994 |

Earns BA from George Washington University

August 7 - Patrick Bouvier Kennedy is born, and dies 39 hours later

After Onassis' death, Jackie returns to New York and becomes a book editor

Daughter Caroline Bouvier Kennedy is born

November 22 - JFK is assassinated in Dallas

Jacqueline Kennedy Onassis dies at the age of 64

Jackie's Final Days

December 1993 - Illness strikes
January 1994 - Doctors diagnose "an extremely aggressive form of non-Hodgkin's lymphonoma"
Recent months - Lymphonoma spreads to the brainand Jackie undergoes chemotherapy
Sunday - Last photograph of Jackie in Central Park

Monday - Jackie is admitted to New York Hospital-Cornell Medical Center and is diagnosed with pneumonia
Wednesday - Doctors conclude that nothing can be done and Jackie checks out of hospital
Thursday - Family and friends gather at her Fifth Avenue apartment - At 10:15 p.m. Jackie dies
Monday - Jackie is buried at Arlinton National Cemetery in Arlington, Va.

Graphic By Joy Gehr

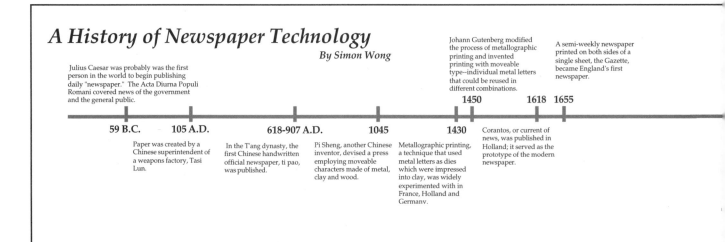

A History of Newspaper Technology
By Simon Wong

Julius Caesar was probably was the first person in the world to begin publishing daily "newspaper." The Acta Diurna Populi Romani covered news of the government and the general public.

Johann Gutenberg modified the process of metallographic printing and invented printing with moveable type--individual metal letters that could be reused in different combinations.

A semi-weekly newspaper printed on both sides of a single sheet, the Gazette, became England's first newspaper.

1450   **1618 1655**

59 B.C.   **105 A.D.**   **618-907 A.D.**   **1045**   **1430**

Paper was created by a Chinese superintendent of a weapons factory, Tasi Lun.

In the T'ang dynasty, the first Chinese handwritten official newspaper, ti pao, was published.

Pi Sheng, another Chinese inventor, devised a press employing moveable characters made of metal, clay and wood.

Metallographic printing, a technique that used metal letters as dies which were impressed into clay, was widely experimented with in France, Holland and Germany.

Corantos, or current of news, was published in Holland; it served as the prototype of the modern newspaper.

Major Dams in the Tennessee Valley Authority System

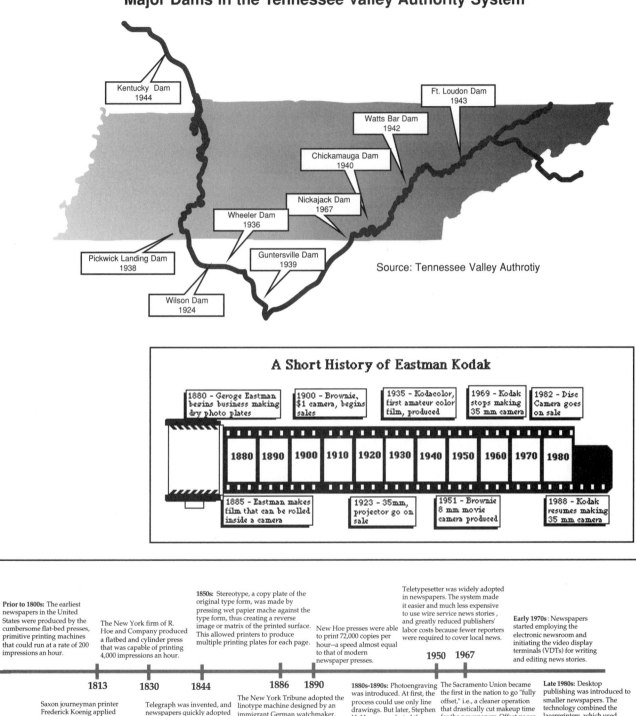

Kentucky Dam 1944

Ft. Loudon Dam 1943

Watts Bar Dam 1942

Chickamauga Dam 1940

Nickajack Dam 1967

Wheeler Dam 1936

Pickwick Landing Dam 1938

Guntersville Dam 1939

Wilson Dam 1924

Source: Tennessee Valley Authrotiy

A Short History of Eastman Kodak

1880 - Geroge Eastman begins business making dry photo plates

1900 - Brownie, $1 camera, begins sales

1935 - Kodacolor, first amateur color film, produced

1969 - Kodak stops making 35 mm camera

1982 - Disc Camera goes on sale

1880 1890 1900 1910 1920 1930 1940 1950 1960 1970 1980

1885 - Eastman makes film that can be rolled inside a camera

1923 - 35mm, projector go on sale

1951 - Brownie 8 mm movie camera produced

1988 - Kodak resumes making 35 mm camera

Prior to 1800s: The earliest newspapers in the United States were produced by the cumbersome flat-bed presses, primitive printing machines that could run at a rate of 200 impressions an hour.

The New York firm of R. Hoe and Company produced a flatbed and cylinder press that was capable of printing 4,000 impressions an hour.

1850s: Stereotype, a copy plate of the original type form, was made by pressing wet papier mache against the type form, thus creating a reverse image or matrix of the printed surface. This allowed printers to produce multiple printing plates for each page.

New Hoe presses were able to print 72,000 copies per hour--a speed almost equal to that of modern newspaper presses.

Teletypesetter was widely adopted in newspapers. The system made it easier and much less expensive to use wire service news stories, and greatly reduced publishers' labor costs because fewer reporters were required to cover local news.

Early 1970s: Newspapers started employing the electronic newsroom and initiating the video display terminals (VDTs) for writing and editing news stories.

1950 1967

1813 1830 1844 1886 1890

Saxon journeyman printer Frederick Koenig applied steam power and developed a printing press with an impression cylinder.

Telegraph was invented, and newspapers quickly adopted it. As a result, journalists could gather and report news information more quickly.

The New York Tribune adopted the linotype machine designed by an immigrant German watchmaker, Ottmar Mergenthaler. Because one linotype machine could do the work of five human typesetters, using more non-advertising material in papers was possible.

1880s-1890s: Photoengraving was introduced. At first, the process could use only line drawings. But later, Stephen H. Horgan perfected the process that permitted photographs to be produced on newspaper presses.

The Sacramento Union became the first in the nation to go "fully offset," i.e., a cleaner operation that drastically cut makeup time for the newspapers. Offset pages were then photographically transferred to thin metal or plastic plates for the presses.

Late 1980s: Desktop publishing was introduced to smaller newspapers. The technology combined the laserprinters, which used xerography rather than photo-chemical, with generic personal computers and software capable of producing text and graphics.

run in the opposite direction from the main line. A block of text explains why this date is important to the chart.

• Pieces of graphic art may accompany this text at various points along the time. These graphics are not usually the main subject of the time chart. They are included to give the chart a more interesting appearance.

The main purpose of a time line is usually to give historical information about a subject. Occasionally, the main point of a time line will be the length of time itself; that is, it will be to demonstrate how long or short a time something has taken. For instance, in the history of the world, the history of mankind occupies relatively little space. A time line would present a dramatic representation of this fact.

BUILDING CHARTS   The charts discussed in Chapter 3 – those in which numerical data form the basis – have some fairly well-defined con-

Chapter review and highlights

• **Process charts:** The general name for charts that emphasize a procedure or the way in which something happens. There are three types of process charts: flow charts, procedure or progress charts, and cosmographs.

Flow charts show movement through some structure or procedure, such as a chart of how a bill becomes a law.

Procedure or progress charts are similar to flow charts, but there are few or no alternatives in the procedure being demonstrated. A chart demonstrating the manufacture of a shirt, for example, would show a flow but there would be no alternatives along the way.

Cosmographs are the only process charts likely to be based on numerical data. Often used with accounting, cosmographs have three parts: input into a processing unit, the processing unit itself, and output from the processing unit itself. Cosmographs demonstrate an organization's sources of income and the amount and types of expenditures.

• **Structure charts:** Charts that take a snapshot of some idea or set of facts as it exists at a particular moment. Their purpose is to show stability. There are four types of structure charts: organization

charts, tree charts, pictorial charts and word charts.

Organization charts show a hierarchical relationship within an organization. It affords the viewer an idea of how an organization is structured and of the relationships among the positions within the organization.

Tree charts are similar to organization charts, but their main purpose is to show relationships instead of lines of power or authority. They start from the bottom up. A decision tree is a specialized tree chart that begins with a problem at the top and presents a variety of solutions and other potential problems.

Pictorial charts are commonly found in newspapers, books, and magazines. They present a drawing or a picture of an object and identify its parts with labels.

Word charts use relatively few words to indicate a much larger set of information. They are often used in oral presentations.

• **Time charts:** These charts use some division of time as the basis for presenting the history of a subject. Its central graphic is a line denoting a time period.

ventions. Consequently, computer software can be developed to help those who would build these types of charts. Not so for the types of charts presented in this chapter. They vary widely in form and content, and the designs must be sensitive to and accommodating of the information they present. The graphic journalist who would build one of these charts must use a combination of knowledge, rigor and imagination.

The journalist must first have a thorough knowledge of the subject matter that he or she wishes to present. Understanding the subject – whether it is the organization of a local company, the history of a subject, or the process by which something happens – is the first order of business for the journalist. As any journalist would, a graphic journalist must find credible and sometimes multiple sources of information. Conflicting information must be checked and evaluated.

In addition to understanding the information, the journalist must also have a firm handle on the forms that can be used to present the information and how those forms can be made to accommodate and enhance the information. A graphic journalist can achieve this understanding by reading about the forms (such as the discussion in this chapter), by observing how others use the forms, and mostly by creating graphics that require these forms. Working with these graphic forms deepens a journalist's knowledge about how they can help with the presentation of information.

Finally, the graphic journalist needs to exercise some imagination in order to picture the information or concepts in a variety of ways. The journalist is not required to invent new forms but should be able to use and manipulate the forms available to give the reader a more complete understanding of the information presented.

FURTHER READING

Willard Cope Brinton, *Graphic Presentation*, New York, Brinton Associates, 1939.

Matthew P. Murgio, *Communications Graphics,* New York: Van Nostrand Reinhold Co., 1969

Anna C. Rogers, *Graphic Charts Handbook,* Washington, D.C.: Public Affairs Press, 1961.

Mary Eleanor Spear, *Charting Statistics*, New York: McGraw-Hill, 1952.

6

Type-based graphics

Type is the most pervasive graphic tool of our society. It can be used with extraordinary efficiency to convey information and ideas. It is so pervasive and efficient that most of the time we do not think of it as an exceptional graphic tool, and consequently those who create informational graphics are likely to ignore its power and versatility.

Graphic journalists should remember that type is the graphic form they will use the most. They should think of type not just as a means of conveying information but also as a way of catching the eye of the reader and sending messages to the reader by the symbolic meaning of the type itself. Type is a marvelously versatile tool, but those who use it effectively need to understand it from the ground up. In this section, we will introduce some of the basics about type.

DEVELOPMENT OF TYPE Men and women from the dawn of history have wanted to make their mark, not just for themselves but for others to see. The story of these efforts and the development of writing and type is one of the most important and fascinating features of the history of mankind.

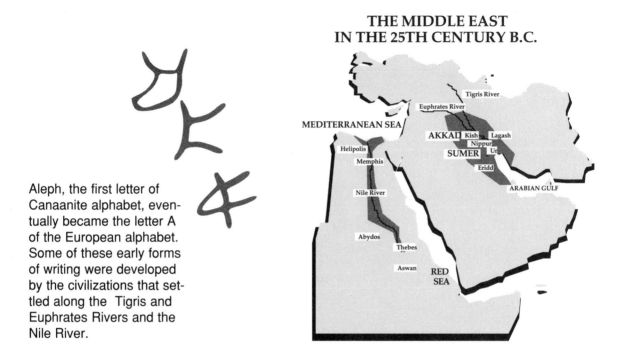

THE MIDDLE EAST
IN THE 25TH CENTURY B.C.

Aleph, the first letter of Canaanite alphabet, eventually became the letter A of the European alphabet. Some of these early forms of writing were developed by the civilizations that settled along the Tigris and Euphrates Rivers and the Nile River.

Early civilizations – groups that gathered together in large numbers to serve as a community – were agricultural and consequently located themselves in the grain producing river valleys of the Middle East and the Orient. The four earliest civilizations spread out along the Nile River in Egypt, the Tigris and Euphrates rivers in Mesopotamia, the Indus Rive in northwest India, and the Yellow River in China. The earliest of these was the Sumerians, who had a thriving society about 3,000 B.C. in the Tigris and Euphrates valley. Part of the maintenance of the society depended on record-keeping, and that necessitated writing. Various means of record-keeping were attempted. Some were more successful than others. The Sumerians developed a stamped seal that could be used and re-used for various tasks. Later they came up with the cylinder seal that is akin to the rolling cylinders of today's printing presses. The Sumerian cylinders, however, were only about as large as a human finger, but they were of great importance in spreading the concept of machinery that could produce messages repeatedly. The Sumerians also developed a phonetic system of writing but were unable to simplify it to a set of single-sound letters. Progress in that area was made by the Egyptians, and they, too, were unable to develop the concept of the alphabet as we know it.

The alphabet that we use today decended from the Phoencians, although it is unclear as to whether this trading society actually originated it. Acutally, a number of civilizations contributed to its creations. Its development, however, represents one of the major achievements in the history of humans. The Greeks adopted the Phoencian system into a set of signs that stood for single sounds of speech, and the Greek alphabet was later refined by the Romans. The 1,500 years that the Greeks and Romans ruled the world (950 B.C. to 550 A.D.) witnessed great advances in the ability of humans to communicate with written symbols. (Writing and printing were being developed in the Orient at the same time, but our alphabaic system does not owe much to those developments.)

Mass producing words, as well as pictures, has always been a necessity among civilized peoples. By the end of the Roman empire, the chief system of doing this was copying, and for a number of centuries much of that was done in the monastaries of Europe and under the direction of the Catholic Church. Letter by letter, line by line, monks would work for most of their adult lives copying ancient manuscripts that the church held valuable. The material they produced was spread throughout the world and helped establish Christianity as a religion and the Catholic Church as the dominant purveyor of it.

It took a thousand years for Western civilization to come up with a more efficient system of reproducing words than copying. That system was movable type, and the name most associated with its "invention" is Johann Gutenberg of Mainz, Germany. Just what contribution Gutenberg made to movable type is open to question because his name never appears in anything that he is supposed to have printed. Still, we do know that around 1450 craftsmen in Germany, possibly including Gutenberg, had put together a technology that revolutionized the reproduction of words. That technology was based on casting single pieces of type into

A page from the Guttenburg Bible

JOHANN GUTENBURG

The man often credited with the invention of movable type was born in Mainz, Germany around 1400. The notion of making multiple copies of something on a printing press had been developed by the Chinese, but because of the large

number of Chinese characters available, it was impractical. Gutenburg was a goldsmith who apparently first experimented with type on a printing press around 1440. It is quite likely that others were involved with the process, but by 1450, his "invention" was ready for commercial use. Gutenburg also developed a type of ink necessary for his new printing process. The only book that we know of that came off his press was the Gutenburg Bible. Because of poverty and blindness, Gutenburg abandoned printing after 1465.

A primer on type

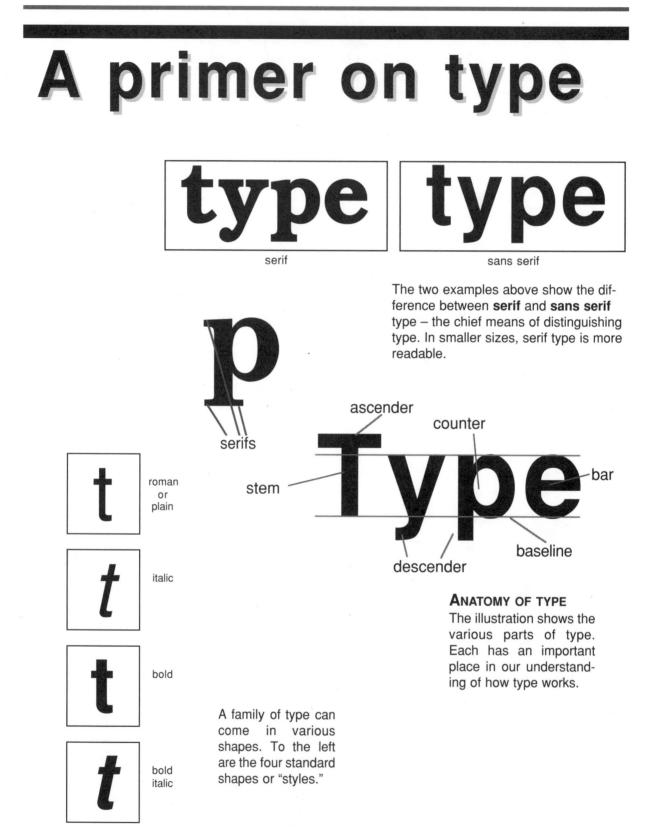

serif   sans serif

The two examples above show the difference between **serif** and **sans serif** type – the chief means of distinguishing type. In smaller sizes, serif type is more readable.

serifs

ascender

counter

stem

bar

baseline

descender

ANATOMY OF TYPE
The illustration shows the various parts of type. Each has an important place in our understanding of how type works.

roman
or
plain

italic

bold

bold
italic

A family of type can come in various shapes. To the left are the four standard shapes or "styles."

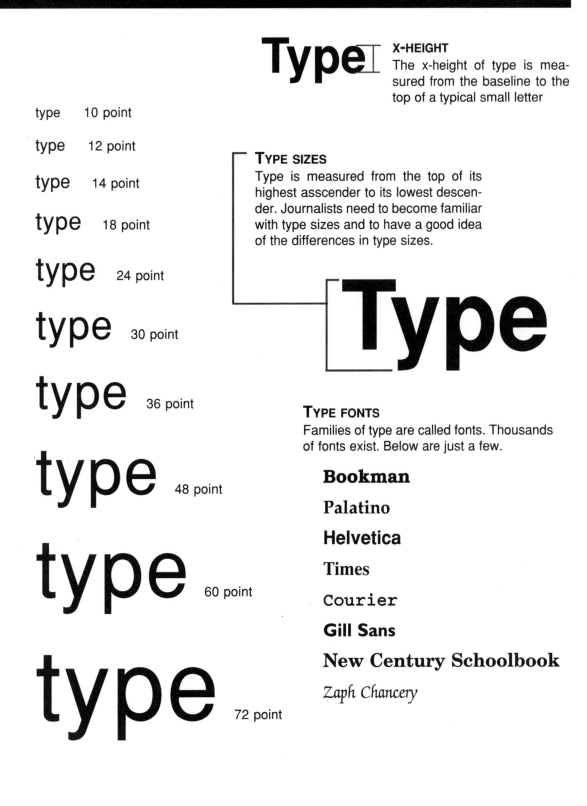

Type

X-HEIGHT
The x-height of type is measured from the baseline to the top of a typical small letter

type   10 point

type   12 point

type   14 point

type   18 point

type   24 point

type   30 point

type   36 point

type   48 point

type   60 point

type   72 point

TYPE SIZES
Type is measured from the top of its highest asscender to its lowest descender. Journalists need to become familiar with type sizes and to have a good idea of the differences in type sizes.

Type

TYPE FONTS
Families of type are called fonts. Thousands of fonts exist. Below are just a few.

Bookman

Palatino

Helvetica

Times

`Courier`

Gill Sans

New Century Schoolbook

Zaph Chancery

whatever combinations were desired to produce, within a few seconds, an entire page of words.

Those single pieces of type were the key to the process that revolutionized our world, and they remain important factors in the work of the graphic journalist today.

ANATOMY OF TYPE Type can have character and personality. It can speak to us in many ways, not just by what it represents in terms of words but also by its own shape and design. Our lives have been enriched by the creation of thousands of typefaces and fonts. Many typographers have devoted their careers to developing type for all kinds of purposes. We owe them a great debt for the job they have done and are doing. Designing a typeface is a tedious and demanding task that requires the typographer to maintain a large vision of his or her goal while seeing to some tiny details. A typeface consists of from 60 to 70 characters that not only must be readily visible as the characters themselves but also must maintain a consistent and distinctive visible motif.

Because of the advent of computers and some specialized software, designing typefaces is easier now than it has been over the past sev-

Leading

The three columns of type below differ only in the amount of leading they have. The columns are set in 10 point type and the one on the left has 11 points of leading, the one in the middle has 12, and the one on the right has 13.

Four score and seven years ago our fathers

Leading is measured from baseline to baseline

Four score and seven years ago, our fathers brought forth on this continent a new nation, conceived in liberty and dedicated to the proposition that all men are created equal.

Now we are engaged in a great civil war testing whether that nation, or any nation so conceived and so dedicated, can long endure.

Four score and seven years ago, our fathers brought forth on this continent a new nation, conceived in liberty and dedicated to the proposition that all men are created equal.

Now we are engaged in a great civil war testing whether that nation, or any nation so conceived and so dedicated, can long endure.

Four score and seven years ago, our fathers brought forth on this continent a new nation, conceived in liberty and dedicated to the proposition that all men are created equal.

Now we are engaged in a great civil war testing whether that nation, or any nation so conceived and so dedicated, can long endure.

Kerning

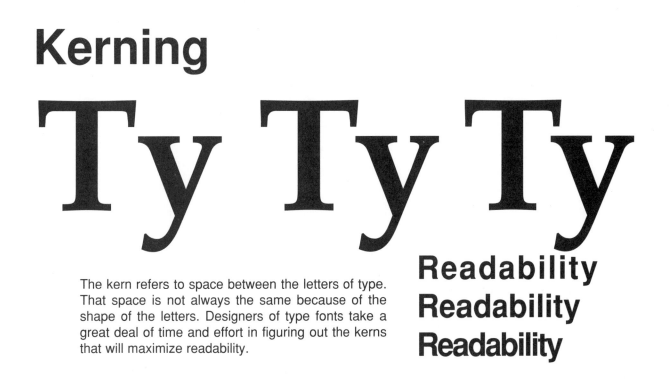

The kern refers to space between the letters of type. That space is not always the same because of the shape of the letters. Designers of type fonts take a great deal of time and effort in figuring out the kerns that will maximize readability.

eral centuries. Still, the good, usable typefaces are relatively rare, and while they can be made with the computer's help, they demand the human touch.

Typefaces are grouped into families, which means that they share similarities. Those similarities include the weight, or thickness, of the strokes making up the type and the width of the characters. Type families may have many different faces, such as bold, extra-bold, roman, italic, bold-italic, and so on.

One of the grand divisions of typefaces is between modern and old style. Modern typefaces are characterized by "vertical stress," that is, emphasis on the vertical lines in the typeface. They have great contrast between thick and thin lines, or strokes. They also maintain hairline serifs. A serif is a small line that comes out from a larger line in a character. The serif is an important part of type that we will discuss later in this chapter. Old style typefaces have small contrast between the thick and thin strokes, diagonal stress, and capitals shorter than ascenders.

Type families may be divided in other ways. One is by the purpose for which the type is being used. Here we have display and body type. Display type is for headlines; it is designed to gain the attention of the reader. Body type for large groups of characters, or body copy, that are not so intrusive in their design. Using a display type for body copy (and vice versa) can be one of the major mistakes that page designers can make.

Another way of distinguishing type is by identifying it as serif or sans serif. As we mentioned before, some typefaces have small extensions at the ends of strokes and are called serif types. These serifs add character to the appearance of the type and often enhance its readability. Sans serif typefaces do not have these extensions. In serif faces, the strokes making up the various characters vary in thickness, whereas in sans serif faces the thickness of the strokes generally does not vary.

A family of type is usually made up of three types of characters: roman, italic and bold. (See illustration on page 96.) In addition, the italic and bold can be combined to make another character, and some typefaces add other characters such as extrabold, thin or light, extralight, semibold, and black. (A "black" character differs from a bold character in that the vertical strokes are much thicker.)

Measurement of type. Type is measured in points; a point is a part of a measuring system that was developed by printers. There are 12 points to a pica; there are about six picas to an inch (and thus 72 points to an inch).

Typesize is the number of points from the highest asscender to the lowest desscender. The ascender is the part of the type that extends above the x-height. The descender is the part of the type that extends below the baseline.

The x-height of type is a very important factor in its readability. The x-height is the size in points of most lowercase letters — those that extend from the baseline to the top of a lowercase x. The x-height of a typeface is one of its most distinguishing features. X-heights can vary greatly from typeface to typeface, and the relationship of the x-height to the other parts of the typeface is important. In many typefaces, the larger the x-height, the more readable the type is at smaller point sizes.

TYPE ON THE PAGE   Type by itself can be studied and admired for its beauty and other qualities, but most of us are interested in putting type to work and in seeing that it does its job properly. In working with type on a page, we are most concerned with a type's size and leading. We may also be concerned with how closely the letters line up with each other. The definitions below and the illustrations in this chapter will help you understand these concepts.

Typesize is the vertical length of type and is measured in points from the top of the tallest ascender to the bottom of the lowest descender.

Leading is the amount of space measured from the baseline of one line of type to the baseline of another line of type. Leading should be greater than typesize. For instance, 10 point type should have more than 10 points of leading to keep the lines from overlapping and thus reducing their readability.

The appropriate amount of leading greatly enhances the readability of a block of type. But what is the appropriate amount? Can there be too much leading? The answer to the second question is yes. Too much white space between the lines can be greatly distracting and as much of a hindrance to ease of reading as too little white space. One rule of thumb is that the leading should be 10 to 20 percent more than the size of the type. The best test of the appropriateness of leading is the eye-of-the-beholder test. When a block of type is set with a particular leading, does it look right? Should there be more or less? With today's computer technology, changing the leading is merely a matter of a few keystrokes. It does not take long to experiment with leading, and that's what should be done if there is doubt. Most software programs that handle type have automatic leading amounts built in. These amounts are generally appro-

Body copy

Which column of type is easier to read – the left column using serif type or the right column using sans serif?
Which headline is easier to read?

Gettysburg address

Four score and seven years ago, our fathers brought forth on this continent a new nation, conceived in liberty and dedicated to the proposition that all men are created equal.

Now we are engaged in a great civil war testing whether that nation, or any nation so conceived and so dedicated, can long endure.

We are met on a great battlefield of that war. We have come to dedicate a portion of that field as a final resting place for those who here gave their lives that the nation might live. It is altogether fitting and proper that we should do this.

But, in a larger sense, we cannot dedicate, we cannot consecrate, we cannot hallow this ground. The brave men, living and dead, who struggled here have consecrated it far above our poor power to add or detract. The world will little note nor long remember what we say here, but it can never forget what they did here. It is for us the living, rather, to be dedicated here to the unfinished work which they who fought here have thus far so nobly advanced. It is rather for us to be here dedicated to the great task remaining before us – that from these honored dead we take increased devotion to that cause for which they gave the last full measure of devotion; that we here highly resolve that these dead shall not have died in vain; that this nation, under God, shall have a new birth of freedom; and that the government of the people, by the people, for the people, shall not perish from the earth.

Gettysburg address

Four score and seven years ago, our fathers brought forth on this continent a new nation, conceived in liberty and dedicated to the proposition that all men are created equal.

Now we are engaged in a great civil war testing whether that nation, or any nation so conceived and so dedicated, can long endure.

We are met on a great battlefield of that war. We have come to dedicate a portion of that field as a final resting place for those who here gave their lives that the nation might live. It is altogether fitting and proper that we should do this.

But, in a larger sense, we cannot dedicate, we cannot consecrate, we cannot hallow this ground. The brave men, living and dead, who struggled here have consecrated it far above our poor power to add or detract. The world will little note nor long remember what we say here, but it can never forget what they did here. It is for us the living, rather, to be dedicated here to the unfinished work which they who fought here have thus far so nobly advanced. It is rather for us to be here dedicated to the great task remaining before us – that from these honored dead we take increased devotion to that cause for which they gave the last full measure of devotion; that we here highly resolve that these dead shall not have died in vain; that this nation, under God, shall have a new birth of freedom; and that the government of the people, by the people, for the people, shall not perish from the earth.

priate so that those using the software do not have to spend time in adjusting them.

The amount of space between the letters of type is another important factor in the readability of type. Adjusting this space is called kerning. When we talk about "kerning type," we are talking about changing the amount of space between the letters. Because most software packages have kerning formulas that have been worked out with the aid of professional typographers, we should be circumspect about changing the kern on type. (One of the most common reasons for kerning is to make headlines fit into an allotted space. That is an easy solution to a headline that does not fit, but it sacrifices readability. The better solution would be to rewrite the headline.) At times, some sets of letters should be kerned, but the reasons should be fairly obvious. Otherwise, the kerning function on a piece of software should be left alone.

USING TYPE   With type as we know it having been around for 2,000 or so years, one would think that some hard and fast rules had been established for its use. Actually, very few rules exist for the use of type. One of those is that we read type from left to right. That rule was settled by about 600 B.C. and overcame the custom of ox-turning; that is, type was written as an ox plowed a field. At the end of a row, the ox would simply turn and plow the next row. Likewise, at the end of a line, the writer would write in the opposite direction on the next line. Beyond our aversion to ox-turning, however, there is very little that we will not do with type, and because there are no "type police," we can get away with just about anything at least once.

A good bit of practice and some research has taught us that there are some things we should observe about the use of type. These are not rules so much as customs and conventions. The following are a few of the most noteworthy of these customs.

Ease of reading. Most of the time, one of the chief concerns in the use of type is that it be easy to read – or at least not totally impossible to read. Consequently, those who use type should let the difficulty or ease of reading help them determine what kind of typeface to use, how large it should be, the width of a column of type, the leading and kerning, and many of the other decisions that need to be made about type. Type is most often used to convey words that have content that we want to get across to the reader. Readability then should be a top consideration for the graphic journalist.

Using serif and sans serif type. In general, we use serif type for body copy, copy where there is a large amount of type. The serifs help lead the reader's eye in and out of type; they give the reader some visual cues that he or she may need to get through a mass of type.

Styles of type

Type can be used in a variety of styles. The most common style is plain or roman. Italic slants type to the right, and boldface thickens the strokes of the letters without changing the basic shapes.

Four score and seven years ago, our fathers brought forth on this continent a new nation, conceived in liberty and dedicated to the proposition that all men are created equal.

Now we are engaged in a great civil war testing whether that nation, or any nation so conceived and so dedicated, can long endure.

Italic type in a block such as the one above is hard to read. Italics should be use on just a few words and for emphasis only.

08	**Oswalt John M** 601 Canyon Cir N 35406	**75**
67	**Oswalt K S** 7025 Hwy 82 E 35405	**75**
18	**Oswalt Larry** 13021 Northside Rd Northport 35476	**33**
98	**Oswalt Lee** 13889 Smokey Hollow Rd Northport 35476 .	**33**
	Oswalt Malcolm 4108 Eleanor St Northport 35476	**33**
34	**Oswalt Malvie N** 2935 Arcadia Dr 35404	**55**
71	**Oswalt Margaret Vidmer** 724 13th St 35401	**75**
41	**Oswalt Michael & Amy**	
03	5851 Hwy 43 N Northport 35476	**33**
17	**Oswalt Mike & Christy** Mormon Rd Northport 35555 . .	**33**
08	**OSWALT MOTOR COMPANY**	
50	8 AM-6 PM Mon-Fri / 7 AM-1 PM Sat	
45	3821 Hwy 82 Nport 35476	**758-**
	3821 Hwy 82 Nport 35476.	**75**
97	**Oswalt Olan** 20187 Hwy 43 N Northport 35476	**33**
67	**Oswalt Orville W** Union Chapel Rd Northport 35476. . .	**33**
	Oswalt P 6800 McFarland Blvd Northport 35476.	**33**

This telephone directory listing shows how boldface type is used for emphasis.

Graphics journalism

100 % reverse

Graphics journalism

black on 20% screen

Graphics journalism

70% screen

Graphics journalism

40% screen

Graphics journalism

20% screen

Other styles of type

Outline

Shadow

SMALL **CAPS**

ALL CAPS

Sans serif type is most often used where the amount of type is small, such as in a label or headline. Sans serif type is also best in larger sizes. With larger typesizes, readers do not need the visual cues to see the type that they need with smaller sizes.

All caps. Copy set in all capitals is more difficult to read than copy set in capitals and lowercase letters. A mixture of capitals and lowercase letters gives the reader more visual cues than all capitals. The all-caps type technique is often use to give emphasis or to note that something is more important or should be looked at before the rest of the copy. A better technique would be to use boldface type to give emphasis to something.

Italics. A block of italic type is harder to read than a block of plain or roman type. Still, italics with roman type give a lot of emphasis to a word or phrase, and that is how they are most often used.

Boldface. Too much boldface is, well, too much. The boldface style of type is used to give emphasis to certain words. That ability is lost when

OBSCURING TYPE
The first rule of using type for informational purposes is to make sure that readers can see it. Obscuring type, however, is not uncommon when people who design layouts are not sure of what they are doing or when they attempt to do too much with the layout elements. In the example on the left, the designer of this brochure did not realize how the picture would obscure the small type on the page.

Scaling type

W   W   W

Computer programs allow users to scale type either horizontally or vertically. The letter on the left becomes the letter in the middle when scaled 200 percent horizontally; it becomes the letter on the right when scaled 200 percent vertically.

everything is in boldface. Not only does the boldface lose its power of emphasis, but it also becomes harder to read than a block of roman type. Graphic journalists should be careful not to overuse boldface or italics styles of type.

Reverse type. Reverse refers to setting white type onto a black background, such as the subheads for this book. Most designers caution against the use of reverse type for two reasons. One is that it is more difficult to read than black type on white paper. The other is that a reverse may not reproduce well during the printing process, and the product could be extremely disappointing.

Neither of these reasons argues for never using reverse. A cleanly produced reverse that uses sans serif type (serif type is even more dangerous in a reverse) can help add variety to a page and can give strong emphasis to an item.

Screens. Even more dangerous than a reverse is type on a gray screen. Unless the screen is fine and the type is bold, the appearance can be mottled and confusing to the reader. A block of type on a screen is especially hard to read. The safest use of a screen is to put a bold, sans serif type on a light screen.

Mixing typefaces. One of the most observed conventions of the use of type is the use of few different typefaces within a publication. Very often a publication will select a typeface for its body copy, another for its headlines, and possibly another for other uses such as cutlines or graphics. Having more than three typefaces that are consistently used in a publication is not considered to be good design practice.

Horizontal and vertical scaling. Many computer programs allow users to change the look of type in a variety of ways. One of the most common ways is horizontal and vertical scaling. This feature lets type be stretched from top to bottom or from left to right without changing the basic shape of the letter itself. Changing type in this way can have some visual impact, but the graphic journalist should take care not to overuse this function because it can quickly lose its power to gain the attention of the reader.

Most of these rules, conventions and practices can be bypassed occasionally when they suit the purpose of the designer or graphics journalist. They should not be ignored, however. They contain some accumulated wisdom about the use of type that needs to be respected. Computer technology gives those who work with type much more freedom than they have ever had, but they need to be thoughtful in the use of that freedom.

TYPE AS A GRAPHIC DEVICE

Type-based graphics are those in which text, or type, is the major graphic element. Sometimes it is the only graphic element. These graphics use type to draw attention to themselves in addition to providing informational content. The following are some common types of text-based graphics.

Drop cap. The drop cap is one of the oldest, simplest, and most commonly used type-based graphics. The first letter of a paragraph is enlarged so that it is seen before any of the other letters of the paragraph are viewed. The drop cap was used in the Gutenburg Bible (see page 95) and has been used in a wide variety of forms ever since. Drop caps have been used for centuries – long before movable type was invented – as a means of capturing the attention of the reader and integrating artwork onto the page.

Lists and tables. Some of the best graphics are nothing more than lists, and lists are readable and popular with readers. They are clean and easy to produce, and they give readers interesting information quickly. A list might be a simple listing of items, such as a movie reviewer's five favorite movies of the year, or it may contain some additional information about the items. Graphically, a list can be paired with some other graphic device such as a set of lines, a screen, an illustration, or even a picture.

A table is a list with additional information about each item in the list. Tables have the advantage of being simple and quick for both the graphic journalist and the reader. They are relatively easy to create, and the white space that they contain makes them easy for readers to locate the information in them. The tabular consists of a headline, a column of categories, and one or more columns of information about the categories. Normally, the column of categories is at the left and the columns of infor-

Drop caps

The main purposes of drop caps are to introduce some typographical variety onto the page and to give the readers some visual cues. On the page, the most striking visual element is the picture of Abraham Lincoln. The drop caps draw the eye of the reader away from the picture and toward the text.

The Gettysburg Address
by
Abraham Lincoln

Four score and seven years ago, our fathers brought forth on this continent a new nation, conceived in liberty and dedicated to the proposition that all men are created equal.

Now we are engaged in a great civil war testing whether that nation, or any nation so conceived and so dedicated, can long endure. We are met on a great battlefield of that war. We have come to dedicate a portion of that field as a final resting place for those who here gave their lives that the nation might live. It is altogether fitting and proper that we should do this.

Lincoln in 1860

But, in a larger sense, we cannot dedicate, we cannot consecrate, we cannot hallow this ground. The brave men, living and dead, who struggled here have consecrated it far above our poor power to add or detract. The world will little note nor long remember what we say here, but it can never forget what they did here. It is for us the living, rather, to be dedicated here to the unfinished work which they who fought here have thus far so nobly advanced. It is rather for us to be here dedicated to the great task remaining before us – that from these honored dead we take increased devotion to that cause for which they gave the last full measure of devotion; that we here highly resolve that these dead shall not have died in vain; that this nation, under God, shall have a new birth of freedom; and that the government of the people, by the people, for the people, shall not perish from the earth.

mation extend to the right; some specialized tables have the categories column in the middle. The categories column is often set off in a different style of type to distinguish it from the information columns. Sometimes a table with a large number of categories will have a screen behind every second, third or fifth category to give the reader some visual cues in looking at it.

Tables can be used to present a wide variety of information. Their main purpose usually is to allow readers to compare information across categories. Tables that carry numerical data might also be turned into bar, column, or pie charts, so the question sometimes arises, "When should you use a table rather than a chart?" The answer may lie with some of the answers to the following questions:

• Is production time important? Tables normally take less time to produce than graphs. When a graphic journalist is working against a tight deadline, the table may be the preferred method of presenting the information.

• Is space a consideration? A table probably requires less space

Lists and tables

Estimated Deaths by Cancer

Oral	8,350
Colon-Rectum	53,300
Lung	142,000
Skin	8,800
Breast	44,300
Uterus	6,000

Most popular gardening activities

Lawn care
Indoor houseplants
Flower gardening
Insect control
Shrub care
Vegetable gardening
Tree care
Landscaping
Flower bulbs
Fruit trees

Source:The National Gardening Association

Game statistics
Super Bowl XXX

Cowboys		Steelers
198	Net passing	207
56	Net rushing	103
50	Total plays	84
15	First downs	25
4	Sacks	2
0	Turnovers	3
26:11	Time of possession	33:49

Counties in Alabama

Name	Established	Origin of name	County seat
Autauga	1818	Indian village	Prattville
Baldwin	1809	Abraham Baldwin	Bay Minette
Bibb	1818	William Bibb	Centreville
Blount	1818	William Blount	Oneonta
Bullock	1866	Edward Bullock	Union Springs
Butler	1819	William Butler	Greenville

Source: *Alabama Political Almanac 1995*

Education expenditures per pupil 1988

Alabama	$2,718
Alaska	7,971
Arizona	3,744
Arkansas	2,989
California	3,840
Colorado	4,462
Connecticut	6,230
Delaware	5,017
District of Columbia	6,132
Florida	4,092
Georgia	3,434
Hawaii	3,919
Idaho	2,667
Illinois	4,369
Indiana	3,794
Iowa	4,124
Kansas	4,076
Kentucky	3,011
Louisiana	3,138
Maine	4,258
Maryland	5,201
Massachusetts	5,471
Michigan	4,692
Minnesota	4,386
Mississippi	2,548
Missouri	3,786
Montana	4,246
Nebraska	3,943
Nevada	3,623
New Hampshire	4,457
New Jersey	6,564
New Mexico	3,691
New York	7,151
North Carolina	3,368
North Dakota	3,519
Ohio	3,998
Oklahoma	3,093
Oregon	4,789
Pennsylvania	4,989
Rhode Island	5,329
South Carolina	3,408
South Dakota	3,249
Tennessee	3,068
Texas	3,608
Utah	2,454
Vermont	5,207
Virginia	4,149
Washington	4,164
West Virginia	3,858
Wisconsin	4,747
Wyoming	5,051

on a page than a graph, and if space is at a premium, a graphic journalist will choose the tabular format.

- What are the differences in the data? If the differences are not great, a chart may not be useful. A good bar chart needs some differences in the lengths of the bars to have some visual impact. If all the bars are the same size, little is gained by presenting the information as a bar chart.

- Are exact numbers necessary to understand the information? This question may be related to the previous one. When it is important to be precise with the information, a table allows such precision. Sometimes a chart will obscure precision.

- Are there two or more types of information to be compared? When this is the case, a chart may confuse the reader. Tables are generally not as visually exciting as charts, but they can present a large amount of detailed information in a manner that is easily digestible for the reader.

- Are the categories so different that the numbers of a chart would be meaningless? Sometimes a table will be used to present information that is not comparable between categories. For instance, a table might present information on two competing companies. It could include the number of employees, the gross annual sales, the stock prices, and the number of plants or worksites for each company. While all of this information is numerical, the figures are not comparable among the categories, and a chart that tried to graph all of this information would not make much sense.

Clear, well-designed tables can be a valuable asset to any publication. A graphic journalist should use a table whenever that is the best means of presenting information. The journalist should not try to make every table into a chart.

Refers. A "refer" (pronounced REE-fer) is short for "reference" in newspaper jargon. It is a way of telling the reader that there is another story on the same subject elsewhere in the paper. It is also a good graphic device that breaks up body type. A refer may include only the page number, or it may have other information about the item.

What refers look like and how much they are used are questions that are usually answered by the style considerations of the publication itself. Some publications, such as *USA Today,* use refers extensively. The design philosophy with *USA Today* is to invite the reader into the publication and to help the reader find his or her way around the newspaper as much as possible. Other publications employ refers minimally. They do so because refers require a good deal of time and attention. The person who creates them must have an extensive knowledge of what else is in the publication, and often this takes much communication with writers and reporters.

The refer carries a heavy burden of accuracy because of their direct use by the reader. The refer should be correct in its summary of the

Refers

Navy jet crashes, plows through homes near Nashville airport

A Navy F-14 fighter jet crashed into a residential neighbourhood minutes after takeoff on Monday, killing both crewmen aboard the plane and three people in a house on the ground, officials said.

The crash ignited a fireball that set three houses on fire in the the middle-class neighbourhood of Luna Heights, sending terrified residents running into the streets.

Nashville Mayor Phil Bredesen told reporters at the scene that emergency workers recovered the bodies of both Navy

F-14 crash

See other stories, page 2

pilots aboard the plane. Their identities were not released, pending notification of relatives.

The other three victims were in one of the houses that caught fire after it was struck by the plane, the mayor said. The house was destroyed, police said.

Two of the three people who died on the ground were identified as Elmer Newsom, 66, and his wife, Ada, 63, emergency officials said. The third victim was a man visiting the couple at the time of the accident, but his name was not immediately available.

David Inman, deputy director of the Tennessee Emergency Management Agency, said the twin-engined, two-seat military jet crashed shortly after taking off from Nashville International Airport at

about 9:30 a.m. CST (10:30 a.m. EST/1530 GMT).

Frightened residents stood near the crash scene clinging to one another while being questioned by police. At least one witness said he saw the body of one pilot still strapped in his seat, and a woman said she saw the plane explode while it was still in the air.

"The plane was coming in extra low," another witness said. "It was obvious there was something wrong with it."

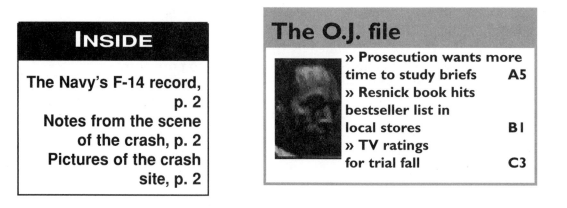

INSIDE

The Navy's F-14 record, p. 2
Notes from the scene of the crash, p. 2
Pictures of the crash site, p. 2

The O.J. file

» **Prosecution wants more time to study briefs   A5**
» **Resnick book hits bestseller list in local stores   BI**
» **TV ratings for trial fall   C3**

article and in the location to which it points the reader. When a reader looks for another article in the publication because of a refer and fails to find it, the reader will be confused – maybe even angry – and the publication will be embarrassed.

Whether they are used extensively or minimally, refers should have a consistent style and placement within the publication. Some readers count on refers heavily to direct them through a publication. They should know what to look for and where to look.

Pull quotes. A pull quote is part of an article that is set off in larger type. It generally serves two purposes: it is a good way of breaking up large amounts of body copy type; it also gives the reader some interesting point or flavor of a story.

Pull quotes are one of the easiest type-based graphics to create. All the graphic journalist must do is select a direct quotation from the article, copy it into another text block, and change the type size, font, and style to conform to the publication's style. That all can be done within a matter of a few seconds. Some thought should be given to the use of pull quotes, however. The journalist needs to have a purpose in selecting the

Pull quotes

Navy jet crashes, plows through homes near Nashville airport

A Navy F-14 fighter jet crashed into a residential neighbourhood minutes after takeoff on Monday, killing both crewmen aboard the plane and three people in a house on the ground, officials said.

The crash ignited a fireball that set three houses on fire in the the middle-class neighbourhood of Luna Heights, sending terrified residents running into the streets.

Nashville Mayor Phil Bredesen told reporters at the scene that emergency workers recovered the bodies of both Navy pilots aboard the plane. Their identities were not released, pending notification of relatives.

The other three victims were in one of the houses that caught fire after it was struck by the plane, the mayor said. The house was destroyed, police said.

Two of the three people who died on the ground were identified as Elmer Newsom, 66, and his wife, Ada, 63, emergency officials said. The third victim was a man visiting the couple at the time of the accident, but his name was not immediately available.

> *"THE PLANE WAS COMING IN EXTRA LOW," ANOTHER WITNESS SAID. "IT WAS OBVIOUS THERE WAS SOMETHING WRONG WITH IT."*

David Inman, deputy director of the Tennessee Emergency Management Agency, said the twin-engined, two-seat military jet crashed shortly after taking off from Nashville International Airport at about 9:30 a.m. CST (10:30 a.m. EST/1530 GMT).

Frightened residents stood near the crash scene clinging to one another while being questioned by police. At least one witness said he saw the body of one pilot still strapped in his seat, and a woman said she saw the plane explode while it was still in the air.

"The plane was coming in extra low," another witness said. "It was obvious there was something wrong with it."

Navy jet crashes, plows through homes near Nashville airport

A Navy F-14 fighter jet crashed into a residential neighbourhood minutes after takeoff on Monday, killing both crewmen aboard the plane and three people in a house on the ground, officials said.

The crash ignited a fireball that set three houses on fire in the the middle-class neighbourhood of Luna Heights, sending terrified residents running into the streets.

Nashville Mayor Phil Bredesen told reporters at the scene that emergency workers recovered the bodies of both Navy pilots aboard the plane. Their identities were not released, pending notification of relatives.

The other three victims were in one of the houses that caught fire after it was struck by the plane, the mayor said. The house was destroyed, police said.

Two of the three people who died on the ground were identified as Elmer Newsom, 66, and his wife, Ada, 63, emergency officials said. The third victim was a man visiting the couple at the time of the accident, but his name was not immediately available.

> *"The plane was coming in extra low," another witness said. "It was obvious there was something wrong with it."*

David Inman, deputy director of the Tennessee Emergency Management Agency, said the twin-engined, two-seat military jet crashed shortly after taking off from Nashville International Airport at about 9:30 a.m. CST (10:30 a.m. EST/1530 GMT).

Frightened residents stood near the crash scene clinging to one another while being questioned by police. At least one witness said he saw the body of one pilot still strapped in his seat, and a woman said she saw the plane explode while it was still in the air.

"The plane was coming in extra low," another witness said. "It was obvious there was something wrong with it."

Navy jet crashes, plows through homes near Nashville airport

A Navy F-14 fighter jet crashed into a residential neighbourhood minutes after takeoff on Monday, killing both crewmen aboard the plane and three people in a house on the ground, officials said.

The crash ignited a fireball that set three houses on fire in the the middle-class neighbourhood of Luna Heights, sending terrified residents running into the streets.

Nashville Mayor Phil Bredesen told reporters at the scene that emergency workers recovered the bodies of both Navy pilots aboard the plane. Their identities were not released, pending notification of relatives.

The other three victims were in one of the houses that caught fire after it was struck by the plane, the mayor said. The house was destroyed, police said.

Two of the three people who died on the ground were identified as Elmer Newsom, 66, and his wife, Ada, 63, emergency officials said. The third victim was a man visiting the couple at the time of the accident, but his name was not immediately available.

> *"The plane was coming in extra low," another witness said. "It was obvious there was something wrong with it."*

David Inman, deputy director of the Tennessee Emergency Management Agency, said the twin-engined, two-seat military jet crashed shortly after taking off from Nashville International Airport at about 9:30 a.m. CST (10:30 a.m. EST/1530 GMT).

Frightened residents stood near the crash scene clinging to one another while being questioned by police. At least one witness said he saw the body of one pilot still strapped in his seat, and a woman said she saw the plane explode while it was still in the air.

"The plane was coming in extra low," another witness said. "It was obvious there was something wrong with it."

quotation. It shouldn't be so inane that it carries little meaning for the reader. It shouldn't be so obscure that it is not understandable. And it shouldn't be so out-of-context that the reader gets the wrong impression about the content of the story from reading it.

An extension of the idea of a pull quote is the quote box. These are groups of quotations that are gathered together in some way on the page. They can work as a stand-alone graphic or as a part of an article where more than one person is quoted. Quote boxes should be designed so that they attract readers and are easy to get through.

Summary and fact boxes

Summaries and fact boxes. One of the best graphic devices for getting information quickly to the reader is the summary box. A summary box can be used on almost any story. It is best used when a story has several parts or important points. For instance, a city council might take a number of actions in one meeting. A summary box can list these actions so that the reader can quickly know what they are.

Summary boxes differ from pull quotes in that they are not taken directly from the story. An editor or graphic journalist must read through the story and summarize a major set of facts from the story. (Some publications require that the reporters turn in summary box material along with the story.) The writing should be succinct and understandable to someone who has not read the story and may not read the story even after reading the summary. The information in a summary box should not single out a solitary but sensational fact about this story; this would give the wrong emphasis to the story and leave an incorrect impression with the reader.

A-3   THE INGLEWOOD CITIZEN, AUGUST 10, 1994

WATERGATE

Sayings produced by political scandal still populate the language

James McCord, one of the Watergate burglars testifies at the Senate Watergate hearings.

Words of Watergate

AFTER burying him with praise just a few months ago, Americans this week remember Richard Nixon's shame — Watergate, the "third-rate burglary" that ended what could have been a first-rate presidency.

As the 20th anniversary of his resignation from the presidency over the Watergate scandal looms, it's time to kick Nixon around one more time for the damage he did to the respect Americans traditionally held for the presidency.

At his funeral in April, attended by every living ex-president, it was a time to remember his opening to China, his flawed peace in Vietnam, his bold try at detente with Russia and his efforts to limit the nuclear arms race.

Now with the anniversary of his resignation on August 9, 1974, it is time to recall a meanness of spirit and a capacity for cover-up that combined to make him the only man to quit the presidency in disgrace.

"What did he know and when did he know it?" was the question asked of the president who had his own dirty tricks squad, his own enemies list, his own bugging equipment, and his own set of grudges and grievances that spread over decades.

That question so infected American public life that it became a litmus test of subsequent presidencies. The acid drip of Watergate made a large hole in the fabric of American confidence in the integrity of elected officials.

It became almost routine for people to wonder about the dirty tricks of the men that followed Nixon into the Oval office.

Did Gerald Ford cut a secret deal with Nixon in return for a pardon? Did Ronald Reagan secretly authorise the sale of arms to Iran to fund Nicaraguan contra rebels? Did George Bush know of the effort by his political appointees to get Bill Clinton's passport records?

Did Clinton play fast and loose with the financing of the Whitewater property development?

The Random House Historical Dictionary of American slang notes that Watergate has given birth to a seemingly never-ending series of scandals called "gates" - - Koreagate, Billygate, and Whitewatergate, to name a few.

Unlike its puny competitors, however, Watergate has lasted in the public memory. The other "gates" slammed shut fast.

The reason may be that there was more to Watergate than just an attempted break-in at Democratic Party National headquarters by a bunch of misguided ideologues funded by a lavish campaign treasury.

The break-in was part of a whole series of illegal actions taken by a president almost paranoid that the world was conspiring against him.

Shortly after taking office, Nixon secretly bugged the telephones of his top foreign policy aides to determine if they were leaking his administration's secrets.

Then with the leaking of the Pentagon Papers, Nixon launched a vendetta against its leaker, Daniel Ellsberg. The "White House Plumbers' Unit" broke into the office of Ellsberg's psychiatrist to steal his notes on what was wrong with Ellsberg.

UNLIKE ITS PUNY COMPETITORS, HOWEVER, WATERGATE HAS LASTED IN THE PUBLIC MEMORY. THE OTHER "GATES" SLAMMED SHUT FAST.

Enemies lists, buggings, illegal break-ins, weird plans to kidnap opponents and firebomb buildings, became the stuff of government.

Watergate stained the Constitution of the United States and left American democracy weaker. It also cut short a presidency of real accomplishment.

Although Nixon never admitted his guilt, on the day he flew out of the White House to his long, lonely exile, he declared: "Never be petty. Always remember others may hate you, but those who hate you don't win unless you hate them, and then you destroy yourself."

As The Times reporter Fred Emery noted in his recent book Watergate, that comment became both Nixon's epitaph and the advice he should have taken before he dispatched his first plumber to fix the first leak of his first administration.

Words of Watergate
What did the president know and when did he know it?
Senator Howard Baker asked this question during the Senate Watergate hearings.

Words of Watergate
... a third-rate burglary.
Ron Zeigler, Richard Nixon's press secretary, describing the Watergate break-in a few days after it happened.

Words of Watergate
... at this point in time.
A favorite redundancy of many of those involved in Watergate. It later became the title of a book about Watergate by Fred Thompson, the minority council in the Senate Watergate hearings. In 1994 Thompson was elected to the U.S. Senate from Tennessee.

Words of Watergate
I am not a crook.
Richard Nixon at a press conference defending his actions in the Watergate caper.

Sen. Sam Ervin (D-N.C.) chaired the Senate Watergate hearings and quickly became a TV star because of it.

Words of Watergate
Follow the money.
One of the chief sources for Robert Woodward and Carl Bernstein, the Washington Post reporters, who first investigated the Watergate break-in was known as Deep Throat because he wanted his identity kept secret. This was his advice to Woodward.

Words of Watergate
smoking gun
Many of the president's defenders often said that President Nixon wasn't responsible for the Watergate coverup because there was no "smoking gun," no piece of evidence that would specifically prove that Nixon participated in the coverup. The White House tapes eventually revealed that there was indeed a smoking gun.

Words of Watergate
Watergate
The word itself is possibly the scandal's most enduring legacy. The suffix -gate has been applied to almost every political scandal since 1974.

Words of Watergate
Saturday night massacre
This was the name given to the firing of Archibal Cox, the Watergate special prosecutor, on a Saturday evening in October 1973. Nixon ordered the firing because Cox would not give up his fight for the White House tapes. Elliot Richardson, the attorney general, and William Ruckleshaus, his deputy, quit rather than give the order to fire Cox.

Except for a couple of pictures, this page contains nothing but type and white space. The designer has used type in a variety of ways to create an interesting and informative page for the reader.

Chapter review and highlights

Two major ways of classifying type
- Serif and san serif
- Body type and display type

What you should know about the anatomy of type:
    styles of type
    type size and how it is measured
    type fonts
    descenders and ascenders
    baseline
    x-height

Types on the page
    Leading: the amount of white space between lines of type
    Kerning: the amount of space between letters of type

General guidelines
Serif type is preferred for body copy while san serif type is good for headlines and display.
Generally, the larger the x-height the more readable the type.
There should be enough leading between lines of type so that the line is readable but not so much that it is distracting.
When setting type in reverse or in a screen, use san serif type

Type-based graphics
    Type offers a wide variety of graphic possibilities: refers, tables, list, drop caps, pull quotes, summaries and fact boxes.

Coming up:
Chapter 7: Illustration-based graphics

Variations on the summary box include the "how-to" box and the "pro-con" boxes. One example of the how-to box is often found with travel stories and describes how to get to the place that is being written about in the article. These boxes give the reader a quick look at information that might be useful.

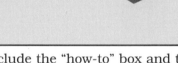 Type may be used purely for attention-getting or decorative purposes. Because type is so pervasive in its non-graphic uses, we sometimes forget its graphic qualities – that is, its shape, form, and weight. Those qualities can have connotative as well as denotative meanings and can deliver a message of impact. Graphic journalists should keep these qualities in mind in producing infographics and remember that type is their most consistent and loyal friend.

FURTHER READING

Edmund Arnold, *Ink on Paper 2*, New York: Harper and Row, 1972.

John R. Biggs, *Basic Typography*, New York: Watson Guptil

Olivia Casey, "Type is to the page as the glass is to the wine," *Design*, Oct/Nov/Dec 1993, pp. 16-17.

Design magazine, Oct/Nov/Dec. 1993 issue; Jan/ Feb/Mar 1995 issue. These two issues are devoted to extensive disucssion of type and typography. *Design* is published by the Society for Newspaper Design and regularly carries articles about type and typography, and a regular contributor is Rolf F Rehe, an international newspaper consultant and typographer.

Alexander Lawson, Dwight Agner, *Printing Types: An Introduction*, Boston: Beacon Press, 1972.

Lewis Blackwell, *20th Century Type*, New York: Rizzoli Press, 1992.

Miles Tinker, *Legibility of Print*, Ames, Iowa: Iowa State University Press, 1963

Walter Tracy, *Letters of Credit*, Boston: David Godine, 1986.

Upper and Lower Case magazine. This magazine is the international journal of type and graphic design, published by the International Typeface Corporation.

7

Illustration-based graphics

Illustration pervades today's newspapers and magazines. Space that once went to photographers, headline writers, columnists and even some reporters has been taken over by the illustrator. Editors compete for the time and talent of the staff illustrator, knowing that an illustration means more space, better play, more attention, and ultimately more readers for a story. Many newspapers and magazines have created or increased the size of their art departments so that many jobs have become available for illustrators. Many of those jobs go unfilled. Whereas once the only person at a newspaper who could draw was the cartoonist, now artists abound.

As with every other part of the publication process, the work of the illustrator has been profoundly affected by the computer. The talents of the illustrator no longer necessarily begin with the ability to draw, although those with artistic bents are the ones most naturally attracted to these jobs. Straight and curved lines can be manipulated easily and quickly on the computer. Screens and patterns can be called in just as easily. Parts of a drawing can be duplicated when necessary in just a second or two. A freehand drawing can be made into an electronic file with a scanner, and then it can be manipulated digitally. Color can be introduced and modified. The list of activities in this regard goes on and on.

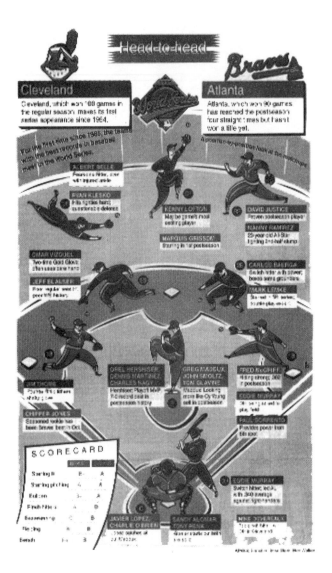

Illustrations play a major part in enhancing information that newspapers, magazines, and newsletters present. They grab the attention of the reader and give the reader an interesting entré into the information. The information in this graphic could be presented in text or tabular form, but interest in it is heightened because of the simple but effective graphic that accompanies it.

Just about anything an artist once did by hand can now be done on a computer, although many artists still work by hand – at least in the early stages of their work.

All of these conditions mean that publications today produce what we call illustration-based graphics. This fifth major division of infographics (after chart-based graphics, maps, charts without numbers, and type-based graphics) is defined as the graphic that uses illustration as the main element within the graphic. Although other graphic devices, especially type may be used within the graphic, the illustration is the major vehicle used by the graphic journalist to carry the information within the graphic.

ATTENTION-GETTING GRAPHICS

Boths of these pages use a pen and ink illustration to draw the attention of the readers to the story. Neither drawing adds much information to the story, but they do make strong visual points.

ALABAMA JOURNALIST

College of Communication, University of Alabama

October 1992

Covering the candidates

Alabama's reporters must run the Secret Service gauntlet

By Barry Wise

As November approaches and election time nears, national candidates make daily appearances at rallies across the nation. These spirited events pose unique problems to the journalists assigned to cover them. Over-zealous Secret Service agents, candidate accessibility and writing truthful stories are only a few of the obstacles that journalists face while covering political rallies.

Journalists in Alabama are no different. Since the beginning of the campaign year, all four national candidates have made appearances in the state and most are expected to return before election day in November. While Bill Clinton, Al Gore and Dan Quayle made brief stops, President George Bush staged a highly publicized rally in August in the parking lot of the Riverchase Galleria in Birmingham.

In trying to cover these stories, journalists often find themselves at odds with security officers and Secret Service agents. "The Secret Service affects coverage very strongly," Ted Bryant, political reporter and columnist for the Birmingham Post-Herald, said. "At a rally, the press doesn't get close to the candidates as a rule. The Secret Service greatly limits access to the candidates."

Bryant recalls a time during the 1984 presidential campaign when Walter Mondale's Secret Service agents shoved him to the ground after Bryant had been granted an interview by Mondale's press secretary. "He just put his hand on my head and shoved," Bryant remembers. "I guess he thought that I was some sort of threat."

Security measures at these types of events are routine and understandably so. Oftentimes, however, journalists experience excessive force by the Secret Service. "The Secret Service can be very pushy and they can be a little excessive sometimes," Tom Gordon, a reporter for the Birmingham News, said. "The candidates seem to want it both ways, they want to be seen getting close to the people but then the Secret Service refuses to let the press get anywhere near the the candidate or the people."

The national candidates travel with full-time security, and are also by a national media press corp. Bush currently travels with a pool of 50 reporters. These national reporters can have advantages over local journalists who don't cover the candidates on a regular basis.

"The presidential press people are more attuned to these people (national media)," Bryant said. Gordon agrees, "There are realistic limitations to what you can do as a

Continued on Page 7

In this issue of the

Alabama Journalist

This edition of the Alabama Journalist is devoted to the issue of politics and the media. In addition, we also have stories about community journalism in Alabama and the College of Communication.

If you have comments or suggestions about what you see, let us know.

A profile of a political cartoonist — Page 2

The Moundville Times — Page 4

Covering politics in the community paper — Page 5

Broadcast coverage of politics — Page 6

A political pollster — Page 8

As elsewhere, Alabama's media depend on the polls

By Simon Wong

"If the election were held today for whom would you vote?"

Sound familiar?

This, indeed, is essentially the standardized question that all public opinion polls ask during election years.

Actually, not only political polls but public opinion surveys in general have become the most popular means to understand the views of the general public about almost any subject matters in recent years.

In Alabama, at least three newspapers have joined the camp of the national media like the New York Times, USA Today, Time magazine, CNN, and the three major networks, to set up an editorial policy of sponsoring their own surveys. These are the Anniston Star, the Birmingham News, and the Mobile Register.

Conducting on a quarterly basis, the Star is joined by a local television station in east Alabama. It covers major issues, political or non-political, and elections on all

Continued on Page 7

The Daily News, September 8, 1993, Page 3

Unbanned

By United Press International

Penn. judge dismisses complaints against book

A Pennsylvania judge has dismissed the case of a Pentecostal minister who wanted the Apollo-Ridge School District to ban an award-winning children's book, "Dragonwings."

Sylvia Hall argued the use of author Lawrence Yepp's book in eighth- grade classes violated the U.S. Constitution because it promoted Taoism, reincarnation and secular humanism. Hall, of Kiski, Pa., said the beliefs were inconsistent with her Fundamentalist Christian faith.

The American Civil Liberties Union argued the case on behalf of the school district.

Armstrong County President Judge Joseph Nickleach ruled Wednesday "neither the book nor the teachers who taught it expounded a particular religion as the only correct belief or even the preferred belief," and therefore did not violate the Constitution.

The ACLU said the judge reaffirmed the longstanding legal precedent that simply discussing in school different religious beliefs in a historical or literary context does not violate the Constitution.

"So long as religious dogma is not promoted in any way nor one's religious beliefs hindered or criticized, the Establishment Clause (of the constitution) is not violated," Nickleach wrote.

The book, published in 1975, tells the story of a Chinese boy who comes to live with his father in Chinatown in San Francisco during the early 1900s.

Hall in May asked the Apollo-Ridge school board to ban the book because it contained the word "demon," a translation of the Chinese word "kuei" meaning ghost or spirit. Chinese characters in the book used the word demon to describe Caucasians because of their light skin.

The ACLU said it applauded the decision.

The civil rights organization said 24 years ago the U.S. Supreme Court struck down an anti-evolution statute and stated a school curriculum could not betailored to satisfy the beliefs of any particular religious group, for that in itself would violate the Constitution.

The ACLU said Nickleach's ruling vindicated that "vitally important principle."

COMPUTER-
GENERATED
ILLUSTRATION

The illustration for this page was drawn completely on the computer using the drawing program Aldus FreeHand.

THE DAILY NEWS

SPORTS

SEPTEMBER 8, 1993

Going for the title

Smith can clinch title with one hit tonight

By Rich Randell

Jim Smith needs just one hit tonight to bring the Bay City Bluebird something they haven't had in 20 years – a batting title.

Smith's average stands at at a searing .335. He is currently tied with the first baseman of the Palatino Pirates, Rod Carney, for the batting lead in the Wine Valley League.

Because the Carney was called up to the Pittsburg Pirates two weeks ago, he will not have another chance to raise his average.

Going into tonight's final game of the season, then, Smith needs only one hit in three or fewer times at bat to pass Carney and take the batting title.

"This is a big deal for me," Smith said.

"Maybe if I can grab the title, that will be something else for the Cardinals to evaluate. That could be another rea-

son for calling me up."

The Bluebirds are a farm team of the St. Louis Cardinals, which has not finished filling out its 40-man roster for September. Smith is hoping to land one of the spots and finish this season in the major leagues.

Smith's manager, Biff Laritino, has vowed to do everything he can to help Smith out.

"As soon as Jim gets a hit tonight, I'm going to pull him out of the game," Laritino said.

"This kid is really something. He has hit consistently all year long. I'm glad that he is in a position to take the title. I am going to recommend to the Cardinals that they pick him up when our season is over," he said.

In addition to his average, Smith has pounded out 20 home runs this year and has knocked in 67 runs, helping the Bluebirds to the best season they have had in more

than five years.

"Jim has been a team player all year long," Laritino said.

"He hasn't worried about his average. He just wants us to win. Tonight is his night, and the team is going to try to help

him accomplish something."

The Bluebirds play the Brighton Braves tonight at historic Kelly Field in the last game of the season. Tonight is fan appreciation night, and tickets are half priced. Game time is 7 p.m., and a fireworks show will follow the game.

PURPOSES OF ILLUSTRATION-BASED GRAPHICS

Infographics that use illustration as their main vehicle serve a variety of purposes for the publication. Sometimes those purposes are interrelated. They include the following:

Picturing what cannot be photographed. Much of life's most important and dramatic phenomena cannot be captured on film. One example of a recurrent and major news event that has never been photographed is an earthquake. Certainly we have seen pictures of the effects of earthquakes – large cracks in the ground and roads, levels of interstate highways sitting on top of each other, buildings that once stood straight now rickety and about to fall down. But the earthquake itself – the thing that caused this damage – cannot be photographed.

Yet, chances are that most of us have a picture of an earthquake in our heads. We can "see" the large masses of land that move against

Caricature

One of the most effective and attention-getting illustration subjects is a rendering of the people in an article, particularly if they are famous people. Caricatures are exaggerations of the physical features of a person, and they have appeared in editorial cartoons for many decades. As publications hire more illustrators, these figures are showing up more and more in many different sections of the publication.

Roger Taney

Winston Churchill

William Rehnquist

Paul "Bear" Bryant

Joe Paterno

Satchel Paige

Isaac Asimov

Bob Dole

Casey Stengel

George Wallace

Mark Twain

each other. We have this picture because of illustrations we have seen that demonstrate what happens when earthquakes occur.

In addition to phenomena that cannot be photographed, illustrations are used to help us envision events that are not likely to be photographed. A plane crash, for instance, is something that we rarely see pictured, even though they occur every day. (As is the case with the earthquake, we often see pictures of the effect of a plane crash.) An illustration can give us a good idea of what happened when a plane crashes. It allows us to "see" the crash even though there is no photograph.

Explaining what happened. Illustration-based graphics are employed to help reporters and editors explain events to their readers. They can show readers the sequence of events. They can let readers see how the parts of an event fit together. They can give readers some idea about the dimension or size of an event, or the elements of an event. Modern journalists understand that explanations sometimes cannot adequately be done with words alone. An illustration can add significantly to a reader's understanding of an event.

Emphasizing points about an event. A good illustration can show readers what is important, and sometimes what ought to be ignored, about an event. It can direct their attention to the things that the writer and illustrator want to emphasize.

Sometimes illustrations use photographs that are staged for exactly this purpose. Publications that use such staged or studio photographs should make sure that readers understand they are not pictures of actual events.

Calling attention to a story. One of the chief reasons for using an illustration-based graphic is to get the reader's attention. Illustrations are considerably different visually from many of the other things a reader is likely to encounter on a page. They often take up a great deal of space on the page, particularly when the white space around them is taken into account. For these reasons they are likely to draw the attention of the reader, and that is exactly the effect they are intended to have. Editors understand that illustrations are sometimes expensive to produce and publish. They should at least have the effect of having people look at them.

Some publications use logos or icons for this same purpose, although neither of these items is likely to take up as much space as a full blown illustration. A logo in the journalistic sense is a small illustration that is often inset into the copy and marks the article as being part of a continuing series of stories about a larger event. Many newspapers developed logos for the 1996 Olympic games in Atlanta and ran them with many of their stories about the Olympics. These logos were often based

A good computer drawing program such as Aldus FreeHand or Adobe Illustrator can give an illustrator a variety of options. The picture above is a pen and ink rendering of a train station. It was scanned and called into FreeHand where it could be screened, such as the version on the right. Below, the illustrator has added shadowing to highlight and dramatize the picture. All of this can be done is a relatively short period of time.

19th century illustrators

A.R. Waud and his sketch
of Lee leaving
Appomattox.

The graphic journalists of today owe a huge debt to the journalist-illustrators and artists of the 19th century who set a high standard of hard work, artistry, and sometimes courage in their jobs.

The most famous of this group are Thomas Nast and Winslow Homer, both of whom were young illustrators sent into the field to help Americans picture the Civil War. Nast did relatively few field sketches that were published but took his impressions back to his drawing board where he produced some fine journalistic art of the war. Homer, like Nast, used the sights he gained in the field to create some of our lasting images about the Civil War.

Both of these men gained their greatest fame after the war – Nast as a cartoonist and Homer as a watercolorist. More important war artists included A.R. Waud and his brother William Waud, both of whom were present at important times of the war to record their visual impressions. The person whose war drawings and paintings we remember most is Edwin

Bunker Hill pictured in *Harper's Magazine*, 1850

Newspaper Row in Washington, D.C.
Harper's Magazine, 1874

The work of 19th century wood engravers shows a remarkable level of skill and subtlety. These engravers illustrated for articles in their publications, but their work and artistry have far outlasted much of the writing in those publications.

Forbes, but he had many peers who produced work of note, namely Conrad Wise Chapman and the Englishman Frank Vizetelly.

Just as important as these and other artists were the craftsmen who worked in the backshops of the day. We know their work, but unfortunately, we don't know many of their names. In the era before photoengraving, these talented people took photographs and sketches and chiseled them into woodblocks that could be used for printing. The process was a tedious one where hurried or care-less work could often be recognized. Yet, day after day, week after week, these people labored on, receiving some compensation but little credit. Their skill brought the sights of far-away places to the eyes of magazine readers, and their work – exhibiting what today is a lost art – shows a feeling and subtlety that is no less than astounding.

A CHICAGO OMNIBUS.

Scribner's Magazine, 1875

MONTHLY MAGAZINE.

LXXXVI.—MARCH, 1874.—Vol. XLVIII.

LIGHT-HOUSES OF THE UNITED STATES.
By CHARLES NORDHOFF.

Congress relating to light-houses was passed August 7, 1789. It pro-
l expenses which shall accrue from and after the 15th day of August,
ary support, maintenance, and repairs of all light-houses, beacons,
iers, erected, placed, or sunk before the passing of this act, at the
n any bay, inlet, harbor, or port
s, for rendering the navigation
fe, shall be defrayed out of the
ted States."
ter, March 26, 1790, the same
cted, but with a proviso that
xpenses shall continue to be so
iited States after the expiration
the day aforesaid, unless such
s, buoys, and public piers shall
be ceded to and vested in the
he State or States respectively
lie, together with the lands and
o belonging, and *together with the
ne."*
tates which possessed sea-ports
supported each its own light-
wo arts Congress prepared to
of these aids to navigation and
onstitution required; and ever
government has not only main-
ed the light-houses, but it has

Harper's Magazine, 1874

umas, "Monte Christo;" Lamartine, "Les | was still his cherished home.
onfidences;" and George Sand, "Con-
e.lo."
In the drawing-room, the candelabra are
ld by the identical gilded figures which
namented the Bucentoro, the barge in
ich the old Doges of Venice went out to

OLD COW LANE, ST. PETER PORT, GUERNSEY.

Guernsey, *Scribner's Magazine*, 1875

The strong illustrations on this page, both hand drawn and computer generated, combine with an open layout and good use of type to have a striking visual effect on the reader.

Logos

on, or included, the official Olympic symbol that was adopted for those games.

An icon is a one-column illustration that is developed specifically for a single article. Good icons go beyond logos and carry some piece of information that the story may contain, and yet they are simple enough to be easily viewed and quickly understood.

CREATING ILLUSTRATIONS
Illustration-based graphics always begin with an idea. An editor, reporter or illustrator will have an idea – usually related to a story or potential story – that he or she decides would be aided by an illustration. The idea itself may come from one person, but it is rarely executed alone. An illustrator will usually consult with an editor or reporter, and each will contribute thoughts or information about what the illustration will contain. If the illustration is to go with a specific article, the illustrator will want to read that article – if it is available – to make sure that he or she understands what the article is saying.

Much of what the illustrator does depends on the amount of time there is to create an illustration. Some articles or story packages are planned weeks in advance of their publication date, and an illustrator may be able to create several illustrations from which an editor can

Icons

These icons were created by Gordon Preece of the Winnipeg Free Press. They manage to give the reader some idea of what the story is about within one column of space. Creating these is no small task, but their eye-catching appeal can attract readers.

choose one. This rarely happens, however. More often, an illustration must be developed over a fairly short period – a week at most and sometimes in just a few minutes.

Most illustrations begin with a pencil and a piece of paper. An illustrator, reporter or editor will sketch out an idea for an illustration. That idea is developed with information and other ideas that are contributed by a variety of people involved with the story.

At some point a computer gets involved with the process. Many illustrators like to produce complete or nearly complete drawings by hand with pencil or pen and ink before they become involved with the computer. This is how most people learned to draw, and they are more comfortable with this method. Once a drawing is complete to their satisfaction, they can scan the drawing and call it into some application such as Adobe Illustrator, Aldus FreeHand, or Adobe Photoshop for enhancement.

Other illustrators begin with just the barest idea – they may bypass the pencil and paper or pen and ink altogether – and go directly to the computer to begin their drawing. Computer applications such as Aldus FreeHand and Adobe Illustrator offer the illustrator a wide variety of tools with which to work, but it often takes a good deal of time and training to master these programs.

Sidebar

PROFILE OF A NEWSPAPER ILLUSTRATOR

Jack Smith

Name: Brad Diller

Position: Illustrator, cartoonist at the *Nashville Banner,* formerly with The *Charleston* (W.Va.) *Daily Mail*

Experience: Began working as an illustrator at *The Daily Mail* eight years ago. Before that, Diller designed advertising inserts for a commercial art company.

Education: Associate art degree from The Art Institute of Pittsburgh

Brad Diller has but one rule for the illustrations he produces: there are no rules.

"I love my job because each time I design something the subject presents unique problems," Diller said. "The colors and typefaces I use depend on the underlying emotional element in the story."

Although Diller concedes that a successful illustrator must be familiar with the basic principles of drawing, he refutes the notion of a consistent style in his work.

His creative process, however, seldom changes. After attending daily meetings with writers and editors, Diller sketches a thumbnail illustration on a legal pad.

"It takes about five minutes to come up with the rough outline," Diller said. "That helps narrow down the theme."

Once approved by his editor, Diller traces the thumbnail and blows it up on a photocopier. That image is scanned into his MacIntosh, where it's saved as a TIF file.

After calling the image into Aldus Freehand, he traces it and tosses the TIF file. The final version is exported as an MS-DOS file and opened up in Quark Xpress in the composition room.

"Sometimes I'll have two days to come up with an illustration, and other times I'll have three weeks."

On occasional slow days at the office, Diller sketches new strips for his cartoon.

Life and lifestyle
in Inglewood

SECTION C
APRIL 22, 1995

AN IMAGE OF OURSELVES

Exhibit of Brady photographs begins in city gallery today

A photograph of the photographer himself just after he had returned from the Battle of Bull Run in 1861.

Story by
Charlie Bender
Illustration and
layout by
Grady Ray Bledsoe

Matthew Brady is the chief source of the images we have of the American Civil War, and according a local historian, he is the chief source of the way in which we look at ourselves.

The citizens of Ticonderoga County will have a marvelous chance to take a look into that mirror beginning today with a major exhibit of Brady photographs. The exhibit includes more than 150 unretouched images tht Brady took during his mor than 30 years of photography in the last half of the 19th century. They include some of the famour photographs that we have seen many times, such as portraits of Abraham Lincoln and a variety of Civil War leaders from both the north and the South.

They also include some rarely seen battlefield images that recorded for history the horror and devastation of the war.

"Brady took an unblinking and unromantic look at the civil conflict that erupted in our nation in the 1860s," David Sloan, a history professor at Ticonderoga College, said. Sloan is the chief consultant for the Hyatt Museum in putting the exhibit together.

"Brady gave us an image of ourselves and that image is not very attractive," Sloan said.

Sloan gives much of the credit for the photographs we have to Brady's assistant, Alexander Gardner, who made many dangerous near the battle lines to take the photographs in the BArdy collection.

"We have forgotten about Garnder," Sloan said, "but we really shouldn't. He took as many photographs as Brady.

The reason we remember Brady, Sloan said, is because of the studio photos of practically every famous person of the day.

"When you were in New York in the 1850s, the 'in' thing to do was to visit Brady's studio and have your picture taken," Sloan said. "Everyone did it, from the not-so-famous to the very famous. Even European royalty knew to drop by."

The exhibit hours are 9 a.m. to 5 p.m. Monday through Saturday, and 1 p.m. to 5 p.m. on Sunday. A reception to open the exhibit will be held at the meusum Thursday night. Admission tot he exhibit is free.

The campaign photograph of Abraham Lincoln (right was taken by Matthew Brady in his New York studio in 1860 when Lincoln traveled there to give his famous "house civided" speech at the Cooper Union. Lincoln always credited the speech and photograph with helping elect him president. At left, the portraits of James Longstreet, Joseph Johnston, Joseph Hooker, and David Porter are typical of those that Brady took throughout his career.

This page combines a strong layout and interesting pictures with an eye-catching illustration to give the reader some additional sense of what the story is about.

Copyright: Swiping ideas without breaking the law

What does copyright law protect?

While ideas or facts cannot be copyrighted, any original presentation of information can be copyrighted. Copyright law protects "anything that can be fixed in a tangible medium." That includes newspaper articles, books, photographs, movies, musical scores, or even a corporation's annual report.

Should I get permission for original works *not* copyrighted?

Yes. Even if a work is not formally copyrighted, its creator can copyright it after the fact and still successfully sue for infringement. Written permission is always the safest route.

What is considered a "fair use" of a copyrighted work?

"Fair use" means that portions of a copyrighted work may be used without permission, often for critiques or analysis of a work.

• Four criteria determine "fair use":

Nature of use: should be educational, not commercial*

Nature of the material: If it is widely available or important material, fair use probably applies

Degree of commercial infringement: If the use won't adversely affect its sales value, fair use applies

Extent of use: If copyrighted material only used to a limited extent, fair use probably applies

What about items in the "public domain"?

Much material exists in the public domain and can be used without restriction. Materials produced by the government, or many materials owned by the Library of Congress is not copyrighted and may be used with a credit line.

When does copyright protection expire?

Generally, material created more than 75 years ago is not protected and is available for unrestricted use.

* Fair use rarely applies to commercial publications. Reliance upon fair use as protection in creating or re-creating i n f o - graphics is dangerous. Even if the graphic is educational or informative, if it is taken from a for-profit publication, "fair use" is not likely to apply.

Jack Smith

Yet another way of beginning an illustration is to start with a piece of "clip art." Clip art can be in either hard copy or electronic form. Newspaper advertising departments often subscribe to clip art books – large portfolios of art work that may include drawings related to food, fashion, transportation, jewelry, seasons and many other subjects. These drawings are usually generic in nature so that they can be used with many different products and brands. Once these clip art books are purchased, the artwork can be used in almost any way the publication sees fit. Clip art is also available in electronic form. Many companies sell a wide variety of images and drawings on a disk or CD-ROM format. Illustrators can begin with these drawings to create illustration-based graphics.

Whether they originate as original hand drawings, clip art or computer art, once illustrations become computer files, they can be enhanced in a number of different ways. They can be enlarged or reduced. Backgrounds, shades and color can be added. They can be merged with other drawings. The illustrator has many options at his or her disposal.

LEGAL AND ETHICAL CONSIDERATIONS

Much of the discussion in this chapter has focused on the creation of original artwork for use in illustration-based graphics. Very often, however, the illustrations used in this way are not created in-house or at least do not begin with original artwork. They may use, or begin with, someone else's work or idea. That is a common practice in many publications, but it must be undertaken with great care and a good understanding of the legal and ethical considerations that accompany the practice.

A graphic journalist constantly asks, "What can I use in doing my work?" Yet a survey of art directors, designers and illustrators published in 1994 in Design magazine showed that two-thirds of them have only a "vague" idea of what copyright law is all about and what they can and cannot use in their work. This lack of understanding can be dangerous. Publications have been sued for large sums of money because they inadvertently violated a copyright. The following are some of the basics of what an illustrator should know and do with regard to using the work of others:

Ideas cannot be copyrighted. This is one of the basic tenants of copyright law. A good idea about a drawing, design, or layout may be used by someone other than the person who created it. Many illustrators keep what they call "swipe" files of good ideas that they have seen that they may want to use or adapt at some point.

But while ideas cannot be copyrighted, the execution of those ideas can be copyrighted. Specific drawings that are generated from an idea may be protected from unauthorized copying. For instance, an illustrator may see a drawing of the Empire State Building used in an illustration comparing it with the tallest buildings in another city. That would be something for her to put into a swipe file. When the time came for the illustrator to create something to illustrate a story about tall buildings in his or her city, it would be an idea that she would consider using. But the illustrator could not use the specific drawing in the swipe file without the permission of the owner. She would have to create her own drawing.

Get permission. This is the first commandment of using someone else's work. An illustrator should have a permission form of some kind in her file that has a place that states specifically what she wants to use and how she wants to use it. Even if a work is not copyrighted, an originator can sometimes copyright it after the fact and sue for damages. Getting permission is the only safe route to take when using other people's work. The permission should always be in writing.

Sometimes, permission will be refused by the originator or the copyright holder. That should be that, and no more consideration should be given to using the work. Sometimes, a fee will be charged for use. In

Chapter review and highlights

The purposes of illustrations
- Picturing what cannot be photographed
- Explaining what happened
- Emphasizing points about an event or an article

Drawing programs
   MacDraw, one of the first object-oriented drawing programs that is still used by many amateur illustrators today; easy to use; quick to get in and out of; very limited in what it will do

   Aldus FreeHand, a high-end drawing program used by many professional illustrators; somewhat difficult to learn but very useful with many options

   Adobe Illustrator, much like Aldus FreeHand and in a race with that application for preeminence among illustrators

19th century illustrators
- They're the ones who started what we are doing today.
- They worked under difficult circumstances both in and out of their offices.
- Many of their names have been lost to us.
- They produced beautiful and interesting works of art, sometimes on a daily basis

Definitions
   Icons, one-column illustrations that give readers some information about a story.

   Logos, small illustrations that are used with articles as identifiers of the type of article the story is

Coming up:
Chapter 8: Avoiding errors and inaccuracies

these cases, the illustrator, editor and publisher will have to decide if using the work is worth the fee.

   The concept of "fair use" can sometimes protect an illustrator in the use of copyrighted material. The doctrine of fair use considers four things in the use of copyrighted material by those who do not own the rights to it:

   a) the nature of the use. That is, the use of the material should be educational rather than commercial.

   b) the nature of the material that is copyrighted. Sometimes the material is so important to the public interest that courts have allowed its unauthorized use. Such was the case in the Zapruder film of the Kennedy assassination. Even though Time, Inc. owns the rights to those pictures, the courts have allowed others to use them because of their importance.

   c) the degree of commercial infringement. The use of material may not decrease the worth of it or will not affect its sales value. In these cases, the unauthorized use of material may be protected.

   d) extent of the use. If copyrighted material is used only to a limited extent, there may be no violation of copyright laws. For instance, some copyrighted material may be included in a presentation that is given to a small group of people. In that instance, the extent of the use would be limited, and there might be no copyright violation.

   Fair use, however, rarely applies to commercial publications, and

A gallery of illustration

Brad Diller

COSMIC BOOM

Scientists at Cornell and several other universities will computer-model the merging of two black holes to test Einstein's theory of general relativity. Einstein's theory predicts black holes should emit celestial signals known as gravity waves when they spiral together.

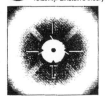

Gravity wave

A black hole is created when a huge star burns the last of its nuclear fuel. The leftover matter collapses into a core so dense that even light cannot escape the intense gravity.

1. The computer scenario begins with two black holes moving near each other in space. According to Einstein's theory, they emit gravity waves, which are ripples in the fabric of space/time.

2. They rotate around each other and merge. emitting intense gravity waves. Scientists will look for this signature with highly sensitive instruments that detect gravity waves.

3. The end result of the model is a larger black hole, which ceases to radiate gravity waves.

Source: Cornell University, Gannett News Service.

Scott Davis/Journal Staff

Scott Davis

King of the Interview

From the president to O.J., everybody wants to talk to Larry

reliance upon it as protection for those creating infographics is dangerous. While a publication may be used for educational purposes, for instance, if it is making a profit, it will be considered commercial by the courts, and the concept of fair use is unlikely to protect it from copyright suits.

Fair use does allow a publication to use copyrighted material to illustrate a story about a person or publication that created it or in a review of that work. Still, it is best to obtain permission for this use if possible.

You may use what you buy. We have discussed earlier in this chapter books and disks of clip art. Many companies are also selling CD-ROM disks filled with pictures. Generally, the images on these disks can be reproduced without restriction, but you should read carefully whatever conditions come with the disks.

Some services are available to find specific items, such as artwork or photographs, that illustrators might need. The Bettman Archive is one such service that specializes in old photographs, drawings and paintings. Images from these services are often sold for one-time use rather than for unlimited use. Illustrators should take care to understand the circumstances underwhich they can use images sold by these services.

A great deal of material exists in the "public domain" and can be used without restriction. Most of what is produced by the government is not copyrighted and may be used in any form. Likewise, much of the material that is owned by the Library of Congress is not copyrighted and may be used with only a credit line. For instance, the Library of Congress has put several of its photographic collections on the Internet, and these photos can be downloaded and used in any way the illustrator sees fit.

Material that was created more than 75 years ago is generally available for unrestricted use. Many old line drawings and wood engravings that come from 19th century magazines are popular with illustrators today. The copyright on these items has expired, and illustrators are safe in using them.

CONCLUSION Illustration-based graphics take a good deal of time and effort to produce, and they often take up a lot of space in a publication, but they can have a lot of impact on readers. They do this by gaining their attention, and then by directing their attention to particular things that the illustrators, reporters, or editors want to say.

FURTHER READING

Daryl Moen, "What's your knowledge of copyright?" *Design*, 52: 22-25, Summer 1994.

Errors and inaccuracy

he chief goal of any journalist is accuracy. The journalist seeks to present information in a context that will allow the reader to interpret it correctly. Most journalists go to great lengths to make sure that their information is accurate. The system of editing that functions at most publications is there to assist in the quest for accuracy. These efforts are made because journalists feel that presenting inaccurate information is professionally embarrassing and will damage their credibility.

Graphic journalists work under the same obligations to achieve accuracy as any reporter or editor. The graphic journalist should make every effort to see that they present correct, up-to-date information in the proper context for their readers. At many publications, however, the efforts to ensure accuracy in graphics have not been as extensive and effective as they are with the written word. Often this is because editors do not understand graphic forms and thus are not able to check a graphic as they would a written story. At some publications, editors may feel that because of the nature of the information in a graphic, there is very little danger of error creeping in. Some publications do not give editors an opportunity to check and question the information that is in a graphic. Finally, some graphic artists themselves do not understand the traditions

A yellow card to the graphic journalist

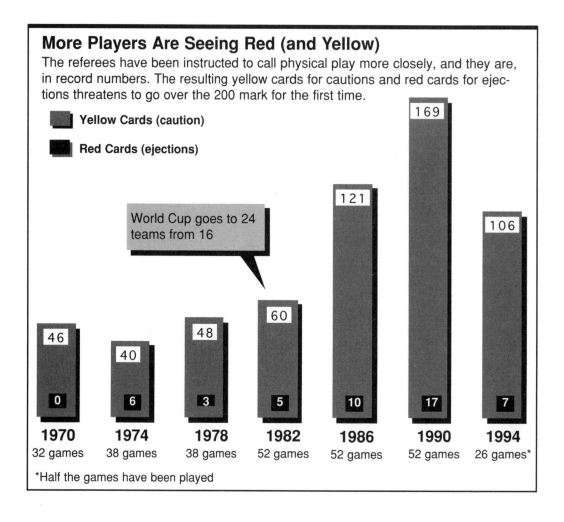

More Players Are Seeing Red (and Yellow)
The referees have been instructed to call physical play more closely, and they are, in record numbers. The resulting yellow cards for cautions and red cards for ejections threatens to go over the 200 mark for the first time.

■ Yellow Cards (caution)

■ Red Cards (ejections)

World Cup goes to 24 teams from 16

	1970	1974	1978	1982	1986	1990	1994
Yellow	46	40	48	60	121	169	106
Red	0	6	3	5	10	17	7
Games	32 games	38 games	38 games	52 games	52 games	52 games	26 games*

*Half the games have been played

and conventions of journalism and do not place a high degree of importance on the presentation of accurate information. They are concerned more with the artistic and technical aspects of developing a graphic and not so much with its informational content.

For these reasons, graphics journalism does not have the best reputation for presenting clear, accurate information. Errors are found in even the simplest charts that contain the most basic of information. They can be found in every type of publication, from the smallest weekly newspapers to the most sophisticated national magazines.

One of the major reasons for this plethora of errors (in addition to the inadequacies of editing at many publications) is that those involved

During the World Cup soccer tournament in 1994 held in the United States, one of the issues concerned the large number of yellow cards (penalties) that were being given to players. A prominent newspaper tried to compare what was happening in that tournament to what was happening in previous tournaments and used the graph on the previous page to do so. The main problem with the graph was that it did not show what it was purporting to show. The graph showed the number of penalties that had been awarded, and while it noted at the bottom of the bars that these numbers were produced in a different number of games in each tournament, that fact should have been taken into account in building the bars. Had the designer of the graph made one calculation – dividing the number of penalities by the number of games played – he or she would have come up with the graph below. This graph compares commonly-based data and does, in fact, show what the designer had in mind to show – that more penalties were being given out in the 1994 games.

Another problem with the graph on the previous page is the placement of the number indicating the number of red cards given at the bottom of the bars. These numbers to not have any relationship to the bars and should not be associated with them.

A final problem with the graph is that the introduction contains a grammatical error.

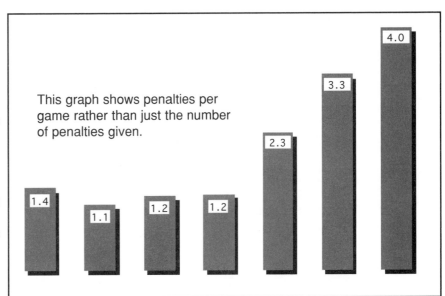

This graph shows penalties per game rather than just the number of penalties given.

with the development of graphics often do not realize how complex and multi-dimensional their job is. They may not understand the conventions of the usage for graphic devices such as the line and pie chart. They may not be able to calculate or assess the numerical information with which they are working. Or they may not be able to understand the proper context in which information should be presented.

Certainly, not all graphics journalists exhibit these qualities. Many are dedicated professionals who understand the difficulties of their jobs and who strive constantly to present accurate information in an accurate context. The entire field of graphics journalism is raising its standards through individual efforts and those of organizations such as the Society for Newspaper Design. Still, the presence of so much error in graphics journalism forces us to to take an unblinking look at this aspect of the work. This chapter will explore the major sources of error that result in inaccurate graphics, the most common types of errors that occur, and some of the practices that can prevent those errors.

SOURCES OF ERROR

Why do errors occur in graphics? A broad view of the field of infographics reveals a wide range of reasons why inaccurate information is presented and why information that is presented cannot be interpreted correctly. These reasons are often related to one another. The following are a few of the major sources of error in infographics:

Inaccurate information. Just as journalists who work with the written word include inaccurate information in their articles, graphic journalists may also include information that is not correct.

One of the chief reasons why information is not accurate is that the sources of that information are not the best. Some sources are notoriously uninformed about the information they present. Those that have gained a reputation for error should be avoided by the graphic journalist. Records kept by local governments, for instance, are simply inaccurate not because of malfeasance or sloppiness on the part of government offi-

What's missing?

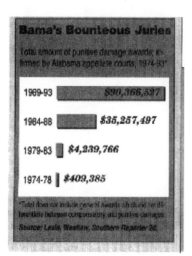

This graph, taken from a retirement assocation newsletter, tries to show how juries in Alabama are awarding much larger punitive judgments in the early 1990s than they were 20 years before. The graphic leaves out some basic information that could have a bearing on how the figures are interpreted. For one thing, it doesn't tell us how many cases these figures are based on. It could be that the number of cases had grown so phenominally that juries are actually awarding *less*. Another factor that the graph fails to take into account is inflation. Dollars in the 1974-78 period should not be compared directly to dollars in the 1989-93 period.

Does it add up?

This interesting and informative graphic compares the prices of the 1995 Thanksgiving dinner to the same dinner for 1994. The problem with the graphic is that the differences add up to $1.25 rather than $1.24.

Big bounty

The average cost of a Thanksgiving dinner rose in 1995, largely because of higher turkey prices.

Average national price of a Thanksgiving meal for 10 people, based on 1995 grocery store prices:

$29.64 up $1.24

(Change from 1994 prices indicated. Prices vary from region to region.)

Whole milk: One gallon
$2.29 down 1 cent

Frozen pie shell: Pkg. of two, nine-inch
$1.29 up 2 cents

Pumpkin pie mix: 30-ounce can
$1.36 unchanged

Whipping cream: one half pint carton
$0.74 up 3 cents

Sweet potatoes: Three pounds
$1.73 up 11 cents

Frozen peas: 12-ounce pkg.
$1.04 up 3 cents

Carrots and celery: One-half pound
$0.61 up 3 cents

Brown and serve rolls: 12-ounce pkg.
$1.24 up 11 cents

Cubed stuffing: 14-ounce pkg.
$2.39 up 13 cents

Fresh cranberries: 12-ounce pkg.
$1.95 up 8 cents

Miscellaneous: Coffee, cream, eggs, sugar, etc.
$2.32 unchanged

Turkey: 16-pound
$12.68 up 97 cents

cials but because of institutional structures that prevent the keeping of accurate records or the impossibility of gathering some information. Voter registration lists are one such example of inaccurate records. In most places, voter registration lists are not purged regularly. People move out of an area constantly, but they rarely inform the voting registrar when they do so. Consequently, it is impossible to calculate with much precision the percentage of voters who vote in any election. The information on voter registration lists is simply not accurate enough to do that.

Even if you put aside the use of voter registration lists and compared the number of people who vote with the number of people in the population, it would still be difficult to draw an accurate picture of interest in voting. Many people do not vote for some quite legitimate reasons. They are unable to go to the polls because they are ill or traveling. Some people are infirm and unable to get to the polls. Registering to vote has not always been an easy process. Here again, we see that calculating a percentage of voting is not a simple matter.

Another reason for inaccurate information is that it is out of date. Graphic journalists generally should use the most up-to-date figures that are available. For example, many census figures begin to lose their value after one or two years. This is particularly true of population figures that are reported every decade. To say in 1996 that a city has a population of a certain number of citizens based on the 1990 census is not accurate. There are probably more up-to-date figures that can be used.

Journalists of all stripes should always question the veracity of information they receive. They should evaluate the sources of that information for their reliability.

Journalist error. Many errors that occur in graphics can be laid solely at the feet of the journalist. Certainly, many of the technical errors that appear are caused by journalists who simply got it wrong. Sometimes this kind of error is due to the laziness or sloppiness of the journalist and his or her work habits.

Other errors occur because of the lack of time necessary to produce an accurate graphic. Most graphic journalists complain about being given too much to do and too little time in which to do it, and their complaints have a lot of merit. Editors often do not understand how much time it takes to create a graphic. They believe that a graphic journalist can make a good graphic instantly with the right computer. (Some graphic journalists may also believe this – at least at the beginning of their careers.)

Nothing could be further from the truth. Producing good graphics, even when using a high-powered computer, can be a slow, laborious practice. Even the simplest graphic can take a long time if the journalist is careful in developing and executing the concept and in checking his or her facts.

Lack of understanding of the information. Sometimes – far too often, in fact – graphic journalists simply do not understand the information they are dealing with. When that happens, they are likely to present the information inaccurately or put the information in the wrong context. Consider the following:

Obscuring the starting point

The annual report of a utility company recently contained a graph similar to the one below to show the growth in the number of its customers. The impression that the graph gives is that the company tripled its customer base in five years. Nothing of the kind happened, however, because the values line of the graph does not begin with zero. A seemingly empty glass on this graph would represent 230,000 customers.

Mixing scales

The graphs on this page commit the all-too-common sin of mixing scales. On one side of the chart the categories mean one thing and on the other side they mean another. In the top graph, the point is to compare the differences (or similarities) between two different stock indices over a period of time. The graph becomes hopelessly confusing when the reader realizes that there are two different scales used in the same graph. The same point could have been made with two different graphs that stood next to each other. The two graphs below do the same thing. They are taken from a government chart purporting to show gain in weight and gain in height on the same graph. Here again, two graphs would be better than one. The designers of these graphs may have mistakenly thought they were being efficient by putting all of their data on one grid. They have sacrificed clarity for effi-ciency.

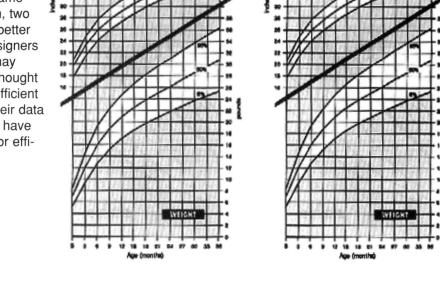

• Stock indexes. These are averages of certain stocks that are traded on a particular stock exchange; they do not include all stock prices, and the numbers themselves are not indicative of stock prices. The numbers that these averages produce have meaning only when compared with previous averages that were calculated in the same way. That is, is the number today more or less than the one yesterday?

What this means to the graphic journalist is that in a graphic of a stock index over a period of time, it is not necessary to show a zero point. An average of 5000 does not mean 5000 from zero; it should be viewed only in the context of other recent stock exchange averages that are calculated in the same way.

•   Earthquake measurements. We often hear that an earthquake "measured 3.4 on the Richter scale." Another earthquake was a 6.1 on the Richter scale. Was the second earthquake nearly twice as large as the first? The answer is no. The Richter scale is not a linear measurement; it is an logarithmic scale, and a 6.1 measurement is far more than a 3.4 measurement.

In comparing earthquake sizes, graphic journalists are tempted to use bar graphs (such as the example on page 145). Such a graph is not an accurate representation of the data. The Northridge earthquake of 1994 was far larger than the graph indicates when it is compared to the San Gabriel Mountains earthquake of 1991.

•   Comparison of survey data. The numbers produced by public opinion polls are often compared directly when they should be considered separately. In most cases, the only survey data that can be accurately compared are those produced by questions worded in exactly the same way.

Here's an example: Let's say that a survey company conducted a survey in 1994 in which it asked the question, "Do you think the amount of money the government spends on welfare should be reduced?" About 75 percent of the sample said "yes." In 1995 the company conducted a similar survey, but this time it asked, "Do you think the amount of money the government spends on the poor should be reduced." This time 75 percent of the respondents said "no." Can we say that in that year support for welfare increased? Certainly not. Most likely, the differences in the numbers were due to the differences in the wording of the questions, not in the fact that people had changed their minds.

Much research has shown that even slight differences in question wording can produce vastly different results in survey data. The graphic journalist needs to take particular care in understanding how survey data are produced before putting them into any kind of comparison chart.

These are three examples where information is commonly misunderstood, and such misunderstandings have produced inaccurate graphics. These examples do not involve obscure pieces of information; they deal with issues and events that we often come across in working with the news. Just because we are familiar with the subject matter does not mean that we understand the information, however. We should be careful about assuming we know and understand these kinds of measurements.

Lack of understanding of charts. Unfortunately, there is still some evidence that those who work with charts and graphs do not understand the conventions of use that we discussed in Chapter 3. Charts are seen by many publications as decorative, rather than information-carrying. A graphic journalist should always ask, "Is this the proper chart to present the information that I have?"

Wrong chart

This neatly designed graphic unfortunately uses a bar chart incorrectly. The data it shows cannot be represented in a linear fashion. Richter scale ratings are measurements of seismic sound waves. A rating of 7.1 is far larger than a 5.8 rating – much larger than can be shown on this graph.

Rattling California's teeth

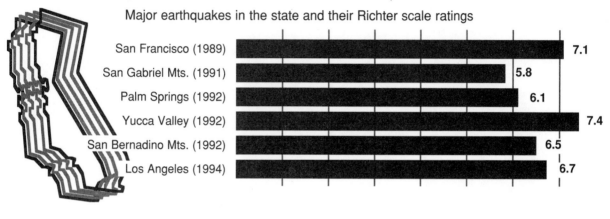

Major earthquakes in the state and their Richter scale ratings

San Francisco (1989)	7.1
San Gabriel Mts. (1991)	5.8
Palm Springs (1992)	6.1
Yucca Valley (1992)	7.4
San Bernadino Mts. (1992)	6.5
Los Angeles (1994)	6.7

Inadequate context for information. All journalists have a constant struggle with the "context problem." The problem is not that sources often claim they were "quoted out of context." The problem, is what do we leave in about a story and what do we keep out? A journalist does not tell everything that he or she knows. The journalist must be selective in presenting information. The problem comes in deciding what information the readers need to adequately understand and properly interpret an article or event.

The graphic journalist struggles with the same problems. How much information is enough? How much is too much? What information is necessary for an adequate understanding of the information in the graphic?

Too often graphic journalists make incorrect decisions about what information to include and what to leave out in their graphics. They do not give the reader enough information to interpret the data correctly, and they leave an erroneous impression of the data.

COMMON PRACTICES Some types of graphic errors occur more often than others. Their recurrence indicates that some common misunderstandings abound among those who produce these graphics. This sec-

Scaling

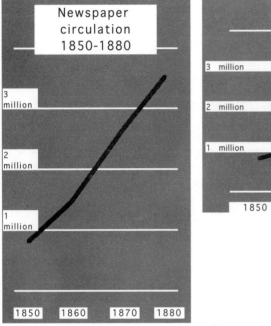

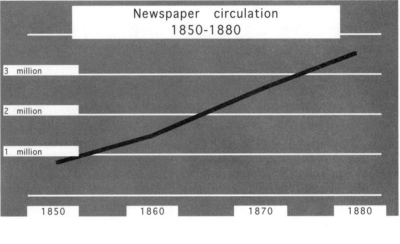

Each of these graphs charts the same data, but they give a decidedly different impression about that information.

tion deals with some of the recurring errors that are found daily in infographics.

Comparing the non-comparable. This practice has already been mentioned in an earlier section of this chapter, but it bears expansion here. Graphic journalists often unwittingly believe that they have data or information they can put into a graph or chart that can be compared and that the comparison will be meaningful. This isn't always so. This type of error has many manifestations.

One of the most common manifestations is the comparison of dollar figures over a long period of time without any adjustment – or without even noting – that inflation has rendered the figures non-comparable. The two charts on page 148 measuring disposable personal income per capita from 1980 to 1992 show what a different picture can emerge when some constant standard is not used. The first chart shows the actual dollars of income while the second shows these dollars measured against the worth of a dollar in 1987. Two different pictures emerge from these charts.

The basic problem in these instances is that a set of figures may not be derived from the same base, and figuring that out may be tricky. Using percentages and rates is often safer than using actual figures. A rate takes a figure and measures it by some common standard. For instance, two running backs in the National Football League may both gain 1,000 yards during a season. Running Back A carried the ball 120 times, while Running Back B carried the ball 150 times. If we wanted to make a meaningful comparison of these two plays, we wouldn't simply graph their total yardage. There would be no difference between the two players. If we figured a rate, however, they would look quite different. We would divide the 1,000 yards by the number of times they carried the ball and find that Running Back A gained 8.3 yards per carry, and Running Back B gained 6.7 yards per carry. That is a substantial difference, and it is strong evidence that Running Back A is a better player than Running Back B – even though they both gain the same number of yards.

Obscuring the starting point or the scale of a graph. Many graphs that appear in newspapers and magazines are decorated by artwork, and sometimes that artwork is fairly elaborate. While some critics strongly object to this artwork (calling it "chart junk"), others believe that this adds an attention-getting aspect to the chart and makes it more inviting to the reader.

The problem comes when that artwork obscures either the starting point of the chart or its scale. Doing either of these things can lessen the chart's value in presenting information to the reader.

Obscuring the data

This graph manages to obscure the data for the serious reader and to totally confuse the casual reader by surrounding it with too much unnecessary and unenlightening illustration. A clean, simple table would have sufficed for this information.

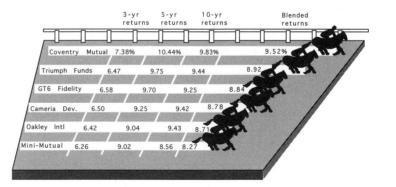

The effects of inflation

Comparing monetary amounts across time is a tricky business, as these two graphs show. A dollar is usually not worth the same as it was five or ten years before, and this fact needs to be taken into account when presenting information such as that below.

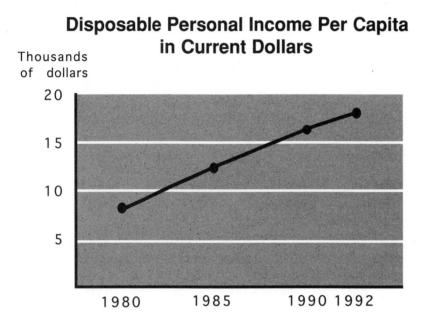

Disposable Personal Income Per Capita in Current Dollars

Thousands of dollars

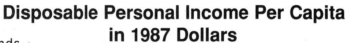

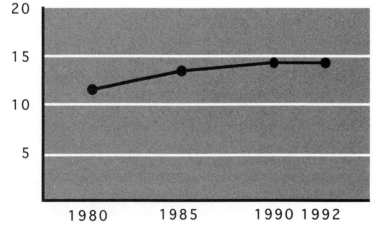

Disposable Personal Income Per Capita in 1987 Dollars

Thousands of dollars

Source: *Statistical Abstract of the United States*

Improper time intervals. Time is something that can be measured, and represented, in consistent intervals. To do otherwise is to misrepresent the data in a chart. Yet this type of error happens routinely. Many graphic journalists feel that if they label a chart correctly, the reader can then figure out that the chart does not represent time consistently. That attitude places form over function and does the graphic journalist no credit.

Scaling. The area of scaling represents not so much error as it does lack of thought about the point of a chart. Should a chart be long or short, big or little? On the next page are two charts that present the same data, and yet the impressions they give the readers about these data are very different. Do the data represent a sharp, steep rise or a slow gentle rise?

Neither of these charts actually misrepresents the data. The graphic journalist must ask, what is the point of the chart? If he or she is trying to say that the time interval represented is here is not a very long one, she would choose the shorter chart. If the time interval in her mind is a long one, however, she should choose the longer chart.

One area is which scaling is not optional is in working with maps.

Proper proportions

A graphic journalist on a major newspaper decided one day that the United States wasn't in the right shape – at least not in the shape that would fit into the space available for the graphic. Presenting a map that is non-proportional is a bad as the non-proportional scaling of a photograph. Journalists have little to do with such distortions in pictures. They should also avoid such distortions in map. The scale of a map should be the same in both north-south and east-west directions.

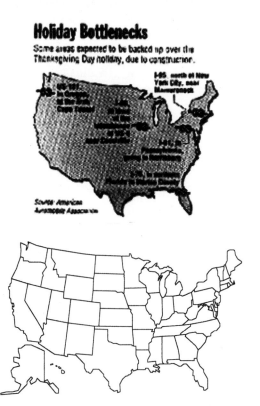

Holiday Bottlenecks

Some areas expected to be backed up over the Thanksgiving Day holiday, due to construction.

Source: American Automobile Association

Chapter review and highlights

Major sources of error in infographics
- Inaccurate information
- Journalist error
- Lack of understanding of the information or data in the graphic
- Lack of understanding of chart forms
- Inadequate context for information

Common practices that result in errors

Comparing the non-comparable. Journalists sometimes try to put data that are fundamentally different on the same chart.

Obscuring the starting point. In most graphs that present numerical data, the starting point should be zero; other material in the graphic should not get in the way of the reader's view of this starting point.

Improper time intervals. A chart that presents time as a factor should present it in uniform intervals even if there are no data for some intervals.

Scaling. Graphic journalists should carefully consider whether or not the scale that they use for their graphics accurately presents the data. Maps should always be proportionally scaled.

Addition and subtraction. Most readers can add and subtract, multiply and divide. The graphic journalist should, too.

Little or no data. Charts and graphics should carry significant data for the reader

Mislocation. Maps should have place names and points as close as possible to where they really are.

Geographic areas should be proportionally scaled in all uses. The fact that a map may not fit well into a given space is no excuse for scaling it disproportionally.

Figures that don't add up. That figures should add up correctly in a graphic is a simple enough concept. There are many times when graphic journalists do not check their sums, and red faces are the result. So they should be. The practice of every journalist who deals with numbers should be to make sure that those numbers make sense.

One particular aspect of this problem is working with percentages. In general, percentages should add up to 100. If they do not, the discrepancy should be explained forthrightly. For instance, percentages that add up to 99 or 101 usually do so because of rounding. Rounding is a legitimate mathematic practice, and a journalist should not try to hide the fact that it has been used by fiddling with the numbers. Sometimes on survey results, percentages will add up to more than 100 because respondents supplied more than one answer to a question. Again, all a journalist has to do in these cases is offer an explanation to the reader.

It is also the responsibility of a journalist to know on what basis a percentage has been calculated. Sometimes, in reporting survey research results, pollsters will discard the responses from those who did not answer the question and figure a percentage based only on those who answered the question. There is nothing wrong with this practice as long as those who look at the data – journalists and general readers alike – know that this is what has happened. Such results are sometimes reported with a "Missing data deleted" note on them.

Charts that carry little or no data. Some editors and reporters continue to think of charts as decorations rather than as vehicles for information. They may request (or demand) a graphic to go along with a story but give little thought to what is in the graphic. The use of charts and graphics in this way wastes valuable publication space and runs the risk of disappointing, confusing or misleading the reader.

Mislocating places and non-proportional scaling of maps. Locating places on a map would seem to be a simple process. Unfortunately, a large number of maps produced by graphic journalists contain mistakes that can be easily caught. Once they are in print, however, the reader is likely to catch them and conclude that the journalist and the publication are not credible.

The major culprit in this area is the journalist's assumption that he or she knows the geography of an area and does not need to check it. An atlas is a terrible thing to waste.

Another problem associated with using maps is non-proportional scaling. Sometimes a graphic journalist will believe that it is acceptable to squeeze or expand a map so that it fits into a space. The same scale should apply to a map whether it is north and south or east and west. Non-proportional scaling or distorting a map in any way reflects poorly on the graphic journalist and the care he or she takes with getting facts exactly right.

When did Nashville move east?

The designer of this graphic moved Nashville nearly 100 miles to the east. The resulting graphic gives an inaccurate depiction of where Nasville is within the state – something that many readers are certain to notice.

Navy jet crashes, plows through homes near Nashville airport

A Navy F-14 fighter jet crashed into a residential neighbourhood minutes after takeoff on Monday, killing both crewmen aboard the plane and three people in a house on the ground, officials said.

The crash ignited a fireball that set three houses on fire in the the middle-class neighbourhood of Luna Heights, sending terrified residents running into the streets.

Nashville Mayor Phil Bredesen told reporters at the scene that emergency workers recovered the bodies of both Navy pilots aboard the plane. Their identities were not released, pending notification of relatives.

The other three victims were in one of the houses that caught fire after it was struck by the plane, the mayor said. The

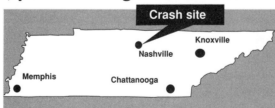

house was destroyed, police said.

Two of the three people who died on the ground were identified as Elmer Newsom, 66, and his wife, Ada, 63, emergency officials said. The third victim was a man visiting the couple at the time of the accident, but his name was not immediately available.

David Inman, deputy director of the Tennessee Emergency Management Agency, said the twin-engined, two-seat military jet crashed shortly after taking off from Nashville International Airport at about 9:30 a.m. CST (10:30 a.m. EST/1530 GMT).

Frightened residents stood near the

crash scene clinging to one another while being questioned by police. At least one witness said he saw the body of one pilot still strapped in his seat, and a woman said she saw the plane explode while it was still in the air.

"The plane was coming in extra low," another witness said. "It was obvious there was something wrong with it."

Witnesses told local television and emergency workers that the jet was flying erratically and low to the ground, and that flames were shooting out the bottom of the plane before it crashed.

Inman said the plane hit three houses. One of the houses was empty, and two people escaped from the second house, he said.

AVOIDING ERROR   Despite the strenuous efforts of the most careful journalists and the most extensive editing systems, errors are bound to occur. Accepting this fact, however, does not mean that we must accept the errors themselves or abdicate efforts to avoid them. Graphic journalists have as much responsibility as any other journalists to present accurate information in a context that will make that information understandable to readers.

The chief safeguard that a graphic journalist has against error is his or her attitude and habits. A journalist should remember the goal of accuracy in presenting information and should always make reasonable – and sometimes more than reasonable – efforts to check information. A journalist should neither think so much of himself that he is always right nor should he think so little of his work to believe that accuracy doesn't matter.

Editors, too, need to hold graphic journalists to the same high standards of accuracy that they require for other staff members. They should put into place systems that will edit graphics and check information in them. Editors also need to be aware of the standard graphic forms and the accepted conventions for their use. Finally, editors should understand that good graphics take time to produce. The fact that a graphic journalist is using a computer does not mean that a graphic can be developed easily or quickly. Like a news story, a graphic depends on information, not form. That information is not always readily available, and when it is acquired, it must be processed and understood by the graphic journalist.

The best graphics are those that are clear and full of information. The journalist owes the reader every effort in getting that information right.

FURTHER READING

W. Daniel DeJarnette, "Looks aren't everything," *Design,* Apr/May /June, 1994, p. 35.

9

Making graphics work

Developing an infographic worth looking at takes time, intelligence, patience, and effort – as well as an awareness of computer hardware and software. Skill and experience are also good traits to throw into the mix. Infographics, like good news stories and feature articles, require a commitment on the part of the publication, not just a few people who happen to work there.

Publications can no longer ignore infographics or assume that it is a minor function to be carried out occasionally and on a part-time basis. The graphic medium is an important and valuable means of communication. Words, headlines and pictures are no substitutes. The graphic stands by itself as a journalistic form, offering things to the journalist and the consumer of news that other forms do not offer. Publications can ignore this form of communication only at their peril.

Given the state of computer technology in the 1990s, any publication that wants to offer interesting and informative graphics that will gain attention, deliver information, make a point, and even entertain can do so. Good graphics are not out of reach for any publication, even the smallest weekly newspaper whose staff does not include anyone with artistic ability. All of us see and learn from graphic forms. We evaluate them just as we do writing and pictures. It is not beyond the skill of any journalist to learn the basics of good graphics and to apply that knowledge when the information at hand calls for it.

A GENERAL APPROACH TO DEVELOPING GRAPHICS

Editors who want to give their publications a more graphic look and who want to take advantage of the things that graphics offer should approach this effort in a thoughtful and serious way. Simply deciding that a publication is going to include more charts and graphs and then appointing someone to develop them is not a productive method and is likely to result in more failures than successes. Even if a staff member is willing to devote the time and talent to developing graphics, that person's production will be limited unless other staff members understand what is being done and are willing to support it. In this chapter, we will discuss some of the considerations that should be made by editors and staff members alike in the development of graphics for a publication.

One of the first principles to adopt is the attitude that everyone who is involved in developing material for a publication should look for graphic possibilities in every article. That is not to say that every article deserves a graphic. Given the time and effort it takes to develop graphics, a publication could rarely meet its deadlines – no matter what they are – if a graphic had to be included with every story. On the other hand, journalists must realize the graphic possibilities in every article they deal with. Then they should be very selective about which of those possibilities they pursue.

The following is a list of some of the graphic possibilities that might be part of an article:

- Any story that includes numbers, percentages or trends;
- Stories where location is important;
- Articles where chronology and context would help the reader understand what the story means; this includes on-going stories and stories that refer to things that have already happened;
- Any story that has a comparison, particularly if the comparison uses numerical data;
- Articles that have information worthy of particular emphasis for the reader;
- Stories that may contain several points that could be summarized quickly in a few words for the reader;
- Articles that contain information that readers need to retain.

This list is just the beginning of the possibilities for the development of graphics. It could be much longer. Reporters and editors should train themselves to think along these lines as stories are being developed.

Another area that editors must consider is the type of resources the publication has to devote to the development of graphics. These resources, first and foremost, include the people that it will take to produce graphics. As good as computers are, they will not produce graphics that are good enough to be included in most publications; people must do that. What people are they? When will they be given time to work on graphic material? Editors must be aware that these are decisions that should be made consciously.

Finally, editors must consider what kind of equipment they have and what they are willing to devote to producing infographic material. Getting into graphic production with inadequate hardware and software can be frustrating and disappointing. Someone on the publication should study thoroughly the hardware and software necessary and within reach of the publication's budget to begin the development of graphics.

MAKING GRAPHICS WORK

Even after giving a graphic much thought, a graphic journalist will find that developing it is, in great part, an intuitive process. The journalist will make many decisions because they *feel* right or because they fit the personal style or preference of the journalist rather than because they are based on some kind of clear logic or research. Understanding that, the following are a few of the ideas that a graphic journalist should have in mind when approaching an infographic.

Consider what graphic form best presents the information. Sometimes this is a fairly simple and obvious matter. A pie chart or a table or a map may be the only choice. At other times, however, the choice may not be so obvious. The journalist will need a solid understanding of all the graphic forms available to make this choice.

Select a point of emphasis. Just as a writer has to decide what an article is about – what the central theme of the story is – a graphic journalist must also decide what the main point of the graphic is. This may be easy in that it is dictated by the data or information the journalist has, but even then the journalist will have to decide what the point of the graphic is.

This point of emphasis is interrelated to the type of graphic form the journalist has chosen to use. A journalist should have a clear idea about what he or she wants the reader to do when reading the graphic. Different graphic forms will accomplish different purposes. For example, the following lists graphic forms and what they are best at doing:

Illustration: draws attention to an article;

Bar chart: allows reader to compare data;

Time line: gives historical overview.

And so on. The key question for the journalist is, "What should my reader know, think, or feel after reading this graphic?"

But my newspaper is too small to have a graphics department . . .

One graphic journalist reports big results at a small newspaper

Being the lone graphic artist at a small daily newspaper can be as rewarding as it is challenging, according to Scott Davis, graphic artist at the *Ithaca* (N.Y.) *Journal*.

"At a small newspaper you have to be creative in using the few resources you have," Davis said. "But it is very interesting because there is a lot of freedom and variety in the job."

The Journal, circulation 19,000, has " a very strong commitment to graphics," Davis said.

While Davis develops locator maps, charts and graphs, others at the paper frequently create "break-out boxes" (pull quotes, statistic boxes and refers).

"Everyone in the editorial department here paginates and can produce some simple graphics for the paper," he added. "That makes the difference."

The Journal staff paginates using Quark Express, and Davis creates all of his graphics in one program; Aldus Freehand. Although time constraints prevent Davis from producing many illustrations, he creates several locator maps and other graphics for each edition of the paper.

Davis' advice for one-man graphic art departments: Be prepared. "If you can build up base maps of your coverage area, you can save time that would be spent scanning."

JACK SMITH

Think of a graphic in the simplest form possible. A journalist should think of the information and the graphic form first and build from there. What is the simplest form in which the information can be presented? After this question has been considered, the journalist can then consider embellishments that should be made from an *informational* and then an *artistic* standpoint.

Many computer programs will allow journalists to do far more to a graphic than should be done. Journalists may feel some obligation to use these programs to their fullest. The trick here is knowing when to stop. Just as a writer should use only the number of words necessary for an article, the graphic journalist should do only what is necessary to accomplish the purpose of the graphic.

Emphasize one or two pieces of information, not five or ten.

Tips for the small newspaper that wants to get into graphics:

Any newspaper or publication of any size can take on a more graphic look. It doesn't take a great deal of manpower or resources. It does take some thought anc careful planning. Here are some tips to get started:

- **Consider first the people, hardware and software that you want to devote to graphic production.** Someone on your staff may be anxious to help produce graphics. Find out what their talents and interests are. Check your hardware. The right kind of computer, photocopier, or scanner is necessary. A few simple software programs, such as MacDraw (or something more sophisticated) and DeltaGraph would be useful.
- **Begin with type-based graphics (Chapter 6).** They're the easiest to produce. Develop a consistent style as quickly as possible.
- **Consider what information you now run regularly that could be put into a more graphic form.** Crime lists, sports scores are prime candidates. Develop a style for these items that you will use consistently. That will save you time.

- **Find a way of digitizing maps of your area.** Put them into a file that you can access easily. You'll be amazed at how much you will use them.
- **Get someone to do line drawings of the major buildings in your area.** If there is no one on your staff, find a local artist or maybe a talented high school student. Run a contest if you think that's a good idea.
- **Collect the logos from the major businesses and organizations in your area.** Scan or photograph these logos and drop them into stories that you run about these organizations.
- **Venture out with a chart presenting numerical data at your first opportunity.**
- **Simplicity: begin doing only what you know you can accomplish in a reasonable time.** It will take time, so be prepared to invest it.
- **Neatness: don't be afraid of white space.** Good use of white space shows that you are a professional and not an amateur.
- **Consistency: develop a style for headlines, labels.** Consistently use a good typeface for these items and don't worry about variety yet.

Many graphics should not be built for the "quick read," although many graphic journalists believe that they are. A good graphic can present a lot of complex information, and there is nothing wrong with a graphic that engages the reader for several minutes, if not longer. In these cases, the journalist would be better off by not trying to emphasize any of the information than by trying to emphasize too many things. A simple, straightforward presentation that gets the attention of the reader may be all that is necessary for a graphic to work. The reader can then take over to consider and digest the information.

Use white space wisely. White space within a graphic is an essential element in making it visually appealing. Even the smallest graphics need some white or empty space to give the reader a visual break. The developer of a graphic should not use up all the space available with strong visual elements that the reader must attend to. One of the easiest the ways to create white space within a graphic is to reduce the size of some of the type. Not all type in a graphic should be the same size. The headline or title should be the largest size, while explanatory

Using white space

son Lake's smorgasl

ıss to stripe to bream, you can catch them all in cho

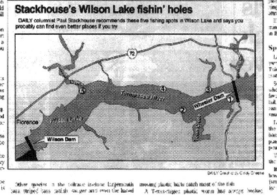

White space can be a good friend of the graphic journalist, but too much white space can be deadly for a graphic. A graphic journalist does not want to fill up every square inch of space available. Some empty space is necessary to give the reader a chance to absorb what is in the graphic. Such space can become dead space when there is too much of it. Both of the graphics on this page suffer from this problem. Each uses too much space without delivering anything interesting and informative to the reader. The map in the top graphic was run across the equivalent of three columns in a newspaper, but there is very little in the map for readers to look at. The pie chart took up two full columns in the paper and said little more than a good headline could have told the reader.

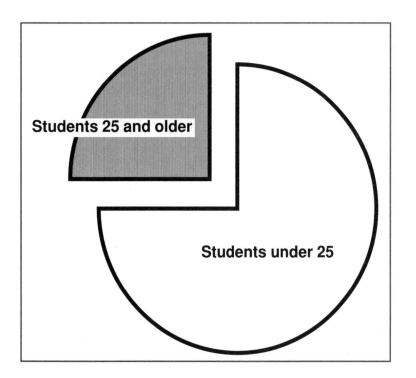

type should be smaller but legible. Labels on elements within the graphic may be smaller. Usually, credits or sources can be the smallest type used in a graphic, and that is where the journalist can save the most space.

On the other hand, too much white or empty space in a graphic lessens its impact. If a reader sees large expanses of empty space, he or she may feel the information in the other parts of the graphic is not very important. An antidote to too much white space is to reduce the overall size of the graphic. A graphic might be more efficient, and have more impact, if it is only a quarter of the size that it was originally created.

Every element should do some work for the graphic. Each part of a graphic should add something to the purpose and the effect intended by the graphic journalist. It should be obvious that an element enhances the informational or visual aspects of the graphic, and that something important would be missing if it were not there.

Develop a consistent style – and a stylebook. Nothing is as efficient as consistency. Writers know that. Graphic journalists should figure that out, too. There is little value in having to think through the formation of a pie chart every time it is decided that one should be used. A graphic journalist and a publication should have a standard form of producing pie charts (and other graphic forms) so their creation can be less wearing and time-consuming. Deviations from the standard can be made when the information or the situation warrants it.

Developing a graphics stylebook for a publication is difficult, if not impossible, to do quickly. The number of graphic forms is too large and varied to be considered at just a few sittings. Some general rules and principles – and decisions about things such as typefaces – can be laid out at the beginning of the process, but the most effective stylebooks are those that are based on the past and current practices of the publication. Ideas and standards can be taken from what a publication has done, and they can be gleaned from the good ideas and practices of other publications. The important thing is that a publication consider graphics important enough to take the time and effort to put together a stylebook. Such a stylebook can help additional people to become involved in the efforts to create graphics.

Keep the reader – a reader – in mind. Many journalists use this technique to remind them that they are writing for an audience of real people. They picture a single reader, someone who is a friend or relative, reading their articles and try to gauge that person's reaction to it.

That's not a bad idea for graphic journalists to adopt. The individual in mind shouldn't be the dumbest or slowest of readers. He or she should be about average. Many of those average readers are being trained by the publications they read to be more sophisticated about looking at graphics and evaluating their content.

Combining graphic forms

It's starting. During the next three years, an army of workers will separate the infamous intersection where four state roads meet. The task is daunting. Utilities will be relocated, new roads and bridges will be created, exisiting ones will be widened and resurfaced, and railroad crossings will be rebuilt. The cost: $27.2 million.

STAGE ONE

The project will be done in three stages. Most of the work for the first stage, which will last until spring 1996, will be done west of the railroad tracks. Here's what will be happening and how it will affect traffic:

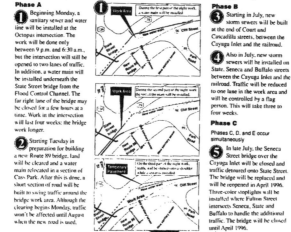

Phase A

1 Beginning Monday, a sanitary sewer and water line will be installed at the Octopus intersection. The work will be done only between 9 p.m. and 6:30 a.m., but the intersection will still be opened to two lanes of traffic. In addition, a water main will be installed underneath the State Street bridge from the Flood Control Channel. The far right lane of the bridge may be closed for a few hours at a time. Work in the intersection will last four weeks; the bridge work longer.

2 Starting Tuesday in preparation for building a new Route 89 bridge, land will be cleared and a water main relocated in a section of Cass Park. After this is done, a short section of road will be built to swing traffic around the bridge work area. Although the clearing begins Monday, traffic won't be affected until August when the new road is used.

Phase B

3 Starting in July, new storm sewers will be built at the end of Court and Cascadilla streets, between the Cayuga Inlet and the railroad.

4 Also in July, new storm sewers will be installed on State, Seneca and Buffalo streets between the Cayuga Inlet and the railroad. Traffic will be reduced to one lane in the work area and will be controlled by a flag person. This will take three to four weeks.

Phase C

Phases C, D and E occur simultaneously

5 In late July, the Seneca Street bridge over the Cayuga Inlet will be closed and traffic detoured onto State Street. The bridge will be replaced and will be reopened in April 1996. Three-color stoplights will be installed where Fulton Street intersects Seneca, State and Buffalo to handle the additional traffic. The bridge will be closed until April 1996.

Phase D

6 In August, new water lines and storm and sanitary sewers will be constructed along Fulton Street, north from Meadow to Court streets. At the point of construction, traffic will be reduced to one lane controlled by a flag person. Work at the intersections of Meadow, State, Seneca, Buffalo and Court will happen between 10 a.m. and 3 p.m.

Phase E

7 In August, traffic will be shifted to the new section of road at Cass Park. In mid-to-late July, work will begin on the two new bridges. The footings for the bridges will be installed, as well as the pilings and the gravel pads. The gravel must settle for three months before the abutments are built. Steel trusses will be installed during the winter, and the concrete work will take place next spring. No work will occur during the Empire State Games.

Stages Two, Three

By October of 1996, both new bridges will be open. In stage two, the Buffalo Street bridge over the inlet will be replaced, Fulton Street will be widened and adjoining streets paved, and Route 13 traffic will split between Fulton and Meadow streets. In stage three, both State Street bridges will be rebuilt.

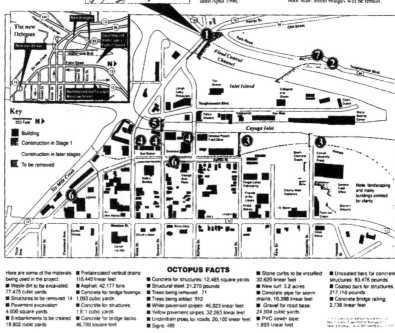

This infographic effectively combines a variety of graphic forms into an interesting and informative graphic that will engage the reader. Understanding the different forms and what they can do gives graphic journalists the ability to make these combinations.

OCTOPUS FACTS

Here are some of the materials being used in the project:
- Waste dirt to be excavated: 77,475 cubic yards
- Structures to be removed: 14
- Pavement excavation: 4,000 square yards
- Embankments to be created: 18,802 cubic yards
- Prefabricated vertical drains: 115,440 linear feet
- Asphalt: 42,177 tons
- Concrete for bridge footings: 1,093 cubic yards
- Concrete for structures: 1,611 cubic yards
- Concrete for bridge decks: 46,790 square feet
- Concrete for structures: 12,485 square yards
- Structural steel: 21,270 pounds
- Trees being removed: 71
- Trees being added: 912
- White pavement stripes: 46,923 linear feet
- Yellow pavement stripes: 32,263 linear feet
- Underdrain pipes for roads: 20,100 linear feet
- Signs: 489
- Stone curbs to be installed: 30,620 linear feet
- New turf: 3.2 acres
- Concrete pipe for storm drains: 10,398 linear feet
- Gravel for road base: 24,904 cubic yards
- PVC sewer pipe: 1,993 linear feet
- Uncoated bars for concrete structures: 83,476 pounds
- Coated bars for structures: 217,110 pounds
- Concrete bridge railing: 2,739 linear feet

Scott Davis, *Ithaca Journal*

News-Sentinel, Sunday, April 16, 1995

OUTDOORS

Olympics come to the Ocoee

e building a river in Polk County

This infographic, like the one on the previous page, combined different graphic forms – a cutaway drawing, a picture, and a map – to give the readers three different views of what the article is about.

Dan Procter, *Knoxville News-Sentinel*

If it doesn't feel right, it probably isn't. This rule of thumb can be very valuable to the graphic journalist. Much of what the journalist does is intuitive and creative, even though he or she may be working with real-world data. The data should not be forced into a form that was not meant to handle it. Data also should not be presented if it is incomplete. Within the graphic itself, information and elements should make sense, and the graphic should lead the reader through them in some logical pattern. A graphic journalist must often trust instinct to tell him or her whether or not the graphic is a good one. Those instincts should be observed and followed.

Evaluate. A graphic journalist should always be willing to cast a cold, objective eye on his or her work – even after it is in print. Sometimes, graphics simply do not work, just as sometimes writing doesn't work. The journalist needs to face up to this fact, particularly after a graphic has been completed. The journalist should ask the opinions of others whose opinions he or she respects. For the graphics that do not seem to work, the journalist should try to figure out why that is so.

PROCEDURES The previous section discussed some of the major considerations a graphic journalist needs to weigh in approaching the job of developing graphics. In this section, we will point out some of the procedures that many journalists undertake in producing their graphics.

Select the software you need and learn it thoroughly. Some people waste a lot of time by buying and trying to learn every new piece of software that comes on the market. A number of different pieces of software are on the market now that will help the graphic journalist produce what he or she needs to produce. The journalist should carefully select only the software that will allow him or her to work most efficiently.

Learning how to use software takes time. The process is more efficient if someone can point out the basics, but the learning comes most quickly when there is a real project to complete and real deadlines to be met. Still, learning a program is not easy or quick, and editors should understand this and be patient.

Finally, graphic journalists should settle on some standard procedures they go through to create graphics. For instance, many will use more than one program to come up with a graphic. A journalist may begin with a chart drawn in DeltaGraph and may export the chart to Aldus FreeHand for enhancement. Then it may have to be saved and called into Quark Xpress so it can be placed on the page. Standardizing these procedures will help the journalist work more efficiently.

Save everything you create. A graphic journalist should have some logical system of saving the things he or she creates that may have some future use. A piece of art that is created for one purpose may be useful in an entirely different project, or a layout or set of specifications that is developed for one thing may be reused in something else. A good clip art file of your own is one of the most helpful things that you can develop.

Constantly look for infographic ideas and information. Ideas about what to put into graphics and how to create them are everywhere. Most graphic journalists have the equivalent of a "swipe file," something that is filled with ideas that the journalist may one day adapt for his or her own use.

Looking for these ideas is particularly important when you travel because you are likely to be exposed to ideas, information, and material that you would never see or notice at home. The graphic journalist should collect maps of cities, airline safety cards, information about buildings, brochures at state welcome centers – anything that might be helpful in building infographics.

Learn to edit yourself. As we discussed in the previous chapter, many of the errors that appear in infographics are there solely because the journalist did not check his or her work. Always add up numbers to make sure they sum correctly. Always make sure that sources of information are credible and up-to-date. Always check locations with a good atlas. Always read the copy inside a graphic with the eye of an editor – or better yet, get someone else to do so. Just as with the other procedures that a graphic journalist does, editing should be standard and systematic.

Write the headline first. Many graphic journalists look upon this dictum as one of the ten commandments of producing graphics. Writing the headline first, before working on the graphic itself, is a good way of understanding what your graphic is about from the beginning. This procedure sets the idea up and gives the journalist the opportunity to execute it.

PRINCIPLES The major principles by which a graphic journalist should abide have been discussed and reiterated in several parts of this book. They can be summarized briefly in this conclusion:

- Graphics should present accurate information in a clear and efficient manner.

- Graphic journalists should understand the many graphic forms and their particular uses.

- Graphics should be information-rich and visually appealing.

- Graphics should serve the purposes of the publication.

FURTHER READING

Scott Davis, "Doing graphics with fewer resources," *Design*, Apr/May /June, 1994, p. 38.

Nigel Holmes, "Nigel on the 'idea machine,'" *Design*, Apr/May/June, 1994, p. 23.

Stephen Kosslyn, *Elements of Graph Design*, 1993.

George Rorick, "Making a graphics department work," *Design*, Apr/May /June, 1994, p. 18.

Glossary

This glossary contains definitions for terms used throughout this book. The numbers in parentheses at the end of the definition stand for the chapters in which these items are discussed more fully.

Accuracy — Always the chief goal of any journalist, accuracy is imperative in developing informational graphics. The graphic journalist must obtain accurate information and present it in an appropriate form for a graphic to be meaningful. (1, 3)

Attribution — Information in graphics should be attributed. While the source of the information is sometimes obvious, attribution may in some cases be vital to the understanding of the graphic. (3)

Axis — Horizontal or vertical lines used to establish values and categories in bar, column or line charts. The horizontal line is known as the *x-axis*, while the vertical line is known as the *y-axis*. (3)

Balance — The design principle that the size of elements within a graphic should not be out of proportion to their importance to the graphic itself. (2)

Bar chart — The bar chart is the most popular type of chart because it is easy to set up, and it can be used in many ways. It uses thick lines or rectangles that run horizontally to present its information. These rectangles represent the amounts of the information being presented. The four major categories of bar charts are: simple, grouped, subdivided and pictographs. (3)

Boldface type — This style of type is used to give emphasis to certain words. Boldface type can be overused, however, and its effectiveness is lost when an entire body of type is boldfaced. (6)

Categories — Chart labels that refer to the items being shown in a chart. Values are chart labels that refer to the amounts of items being shown in the chart. (3)

Clarity — Graphic journalists must always abide by this principle when developing charts. Clarity refers to what readers do with the information presented and whether it is cleanly designed and understandable. (3)

Chart-based graphics — Graphics that present numerical information in a non-text form. These forms are likely to be proportional representations of the numbers themselves. Such charts commonly serve a dual purpose; to show amounts and to show relationships. Accuracy and clarity are key elements of these charts. (3)

Chloropleth map — This map puts various geographic areas into different colors or shadings, and a legend explains what the different shadings mean. Usually, the shadings represent statistical differences. One convention of these maps that is not always observed is that areas in white are not represented by any data. (4)

Column chart — Bar charts in which the bars run vertically. The column chart is most commonly used when time is an element in the data being presented or the relationships being presented. The most common column charts are: simple, grouped, stacked and range. (3)

Consistency — Consistency in graphic items such as type, color and attribution makes reading more efficient, while helping a publication establish a relationship with its readers. (3)

Contrast — A design element using combinations of very light and very dark elements to draw the reader's attention to points of emphasis on a graphic. (2)

Cosmograph — A process chart that is most likely to be based on numerical data. It has three parts: input into a processing unit, the processing unit itself, and output from the processing unit. Most often used with accounting, it can chart the amount and sources of income into an organization and the amount and types of expenditures the organization makes. (5)

Data map — This type of map places numerical data on geographic locations in a way that will produce relevant information about the data. They allow readers to view large amounts of information at a single sighting in an orderly and logical way. Three types of data maps are available: shaded or chloropleth maps, dot maps and isoline maps. (4)

Depth — Created by adding a side or two to the objects in a graph to make them appear as if they are coming off the page. Depth and perspective are the two elements necessary for the object to appear three dimensional. Depth can also be created by shadowing, which involves putting a shaded shape behind the element. (2, 3)

Dot map — A map that uses dots or some other symbol to represent the geographic distribution of something. Dot maps avoid the problem of shaded maps by depending not so much on political divisions as geographic locations. (4)

Fair use — The concept that a portion of another's work, even if copyrighted, may be used without permission. Fair use rarely applies to commercial publications, however, and reliance upon it for protection in borrowing infographics is dangerous. The doctrine of fair use requires four things for protection: the nature of the use must be educational rather than commercial; the nature and importance of the material; the degree of commercial infringement; and extent of the use.(7)

Flow chart — This chart shows some movement through some structure or procedure. The steps in this movement can present alternatives. A flow chart that high school students may be familiar with depicts how a bill becomes a law. The flow chart helps the reader understand how a bill can be changed, killed or re-routed. Such charts use a linear flow, often represented by a single line or arrow. (5)

Focus — A concentration of ink or color in a graphic intended to draw the reader to a point of emphasis. (2)

Grouped bar charts — These bar charts show both amounts and relationships by grouping bars to together. This allows comparisons within one particular group and between other groups. (3)

Headlines — Headlines accompanying graphics do not have to follow the same rules for headlines as articles. In most cases, they can simply be labels without verbs, but they should identify the central idea of the graphic. Some graphic journalists advise that the headline should be written first, allowing the artist to understand exactly what he or she is trying to convey. (3)

Icon — A one-column illustration developed specifically for a single article. Quality icons go beyond logos and can carry some piece of information the story may contain, but they are simple enough to be quickly viewed and easily understood. (7)

Illustration-based graphics— Graphics that use illustration as the main element within the graphic. Although other graphic devices, such as type, may be used within the graphic, the illustration itself drives the graphic. (7)

Isoline maps — Maps that use lines to present data to the reader. The most common isoline map found today is the weather map, which shows temperature variations and the movement of fronts and pressure systems with lines. (4)

Italic type — A block of this type is harder to read than a block of plain or roman type, but italics with roman type can give a lot of emphasis to a word or phrase. (6)

Kerning — The process of adjusting the space between letters of type within a word. Most software packages have kerning formulas developed by professional typographers. At times, some sets of letters should be kerned, but the kerning function should otherwise be left alone. (6)

Labels — Labels are used to identify certain parts of a chart. Two of the most common labels are categories and values, which refer to what and how much is being shown. A label can be put on any element of a chart, but the obvious should not be labeled. Too many labels can be irritating and confusing. (3)

Leading — The amount of space measured from the baseline of one line of type to the baseline of another line of type. Generally, leading should be greater than typesize to prevent the lines from overlapping and losing their readability. It should be 10 to 20 percent bigger than the type size. (6)

Legend — A grouping of text and symbols that helps the reader identify the symbols that are used in a chart. Legends are often imperative for the reader to understand the graphic. They are often presented in a box, and they must be placed in an area that does not obscure any of the chart's data. Legends are not necessary when a chart uses a symbol that is only used once and can be labeled directly.

Line chart — This chart's specific purpose is to show changes in an amount of something over a period of time. In some instances, it is preferable to the bar chart because it is cleaner and easier to decipher. One of the standard conventions of the line chart is that the x-axis represents time and the y-axis represents amounts or quantities being shown. The central idea of the line chart is the shape or direction of the lines in the chart, not the individual plotting points on the line. Types of line charts include simple line, multiple line, area or surface and band charts. (3)

Locator map — The chief purpose of this map is to help the reader locate the places referred to in an article. These maps are usually either flat or relief maps. Flat maps do not show any topographical variations such as hills, valleys and mountains. Relief maps show such variations using a third dimension. (4)

Organization chart — One of the most common charts readers may encounter, this chart shows the hierarchical relationships within an organization at a given time. The key to its effectiveness is its simplicity. It allows the viewer to quickly understand an organization's structure and the relationships among its various positions. (5)

Perspective — An artistic technique that controls the viewpoint of the viewer toward the graphic. Perspective is based on the observation that the closer something is to us, the larger it is. As an object gets farther away, its actual size does not diminish, although our perception of it does. An object will diminish to the vanishing point, a point located on the horizon line where the object can no longer be seen. (2)

Pictograph — Rather than using bars to represent an item, a pictograph uses symbols to represent the item. It is an old fashioned form of a bar chart, but is still popular in many publications today. These can be effective if the symbols are clear and self-explanatory. (3)

Pictorial charts — One of the most common structure charts found in newspapers, magazines and books. It represents a drawing or picture of an object and identifies its parts with labels. Pictoral charts rely heavily on a graphic representation of an object. Although it may describe the process or function of an object with words, the graphic does not show it. The cutaway technique is often used in creating this type of chart. (5)

Pie charts — Also known as the circle chart, these popular charts are used to show how one entity or item is divided up. The divisions shown in pie charts are most commonly expressed in percentages that add up to 100, and only one set of data can be shown at a time. One general rule governing pie charts is that the first "cut" of the pie is made from the center of the circle to the top, or the 12 o'clock position. (3)

Procedure chart — Also known as a process chart, this chart is in many ways like the flow chart. The major difference between a procedure and a flow chart is that what is being presented has few or no alternatives in the procedure. A chart depicting how a shirt is made would, for example, indicate no alternatives in the process. (5)

Process chart — The general name given to a chart that emphasizes some procedure or the way in which something happens. These charts show some movement or dynamic process. There are three types of process charts: flow charts, procedure or progress charts, and cosmographs. (5)

Proportionality — The concept that graphic forms must be physically proportional when representing numerical data. Proportionality is easiest to achieve when there is only one dimension involved in the graphic. Achieving proportionality becomes more difficult when a third dimension is introduced or when objects are taken off a flat plane. (2)

Pull quote — Part of an article that is set off in larger type. Pull quotes generally serve two purposes: breaking up large amounts of body copy type; and giving the reader some interesting point or flavor from the story. (6)

Range bar chart — This type of chart is useful in showing sets of information that fluctuate and in allowing viewers to compare those sets. They show maximum and minimum values for each item or time period represented. (3)

Refer — Short for "reference" in newspaper jargon, a refer is a text-based graphic that tells the reader there is another story on the same subject elsewhere in the paper. This graphic device is a good means of breaking up body type. It may include only the page number, or it may have other information about the item. (6)

Sans serif type — Type faces that do not have small extensions, known as serifs, at the end of a character's strokes. In sans serif type, the thickness of the strokes that make up the characters generally does not vary. This type is generally used when a larger type size is needed for smaller amounts of copy. (6)

Serif type — Type faces that have small extensions, or lines, at the end of a character's strokes. These "serifs" add character to the appearance of type and often enhance its readability. In serif type, the strokes that make up the various characters vary in thickness. Serif type is generally used for smaller body copy, because the serifs provide visual cues for the reader's eyes while they move through a mass of type. (6)

Simple bar chart — These charts use single horizontal bars to represent different values of one thing. Simple bar charts can be set up and manipulated with relative ease. (3)

Simple column chart — These charts typically depict values of one category over a period of time. This graphic is popular because it is easy to create and easy for the reader to understand. (3)

Simplicity — The principle that a graphic should contain the minimum items necessary for the reader to understand the information and the maximum items for good appearance. (3)

Spikes — Abberations in a line chart's data that are likely to throw the chart's line out of kilter. Sometimes spikes can be broken so that the shape of the chart is not completely damaged. (3)

Structure charts — These charts take a snapshot of some idea or set of facts as they exist at a particular moment. Their purpose is to show stability. There are four types of structure charts: organization charts, tree charts, pictorial charts and word charts. (5)

Subdivided bar chart — A single subdivided bar shows how something is divided, and the values can be expressed in absolute numbers or percentages. (3)

Time charts — Sometimes called time lines, these charts provide historical information that allows the viewer to put the situation or subject being presented into a context. It uses some division of time as the basis for constructing the chart, and the central graphic element is a line denoting a time period. The line can run vertically or horizontally, depending on the needs of the graphic journalist. (5)

Tree charts — Based on a visual chart that represents the branches of a tree, this chart is similar to the organization chart. Its main purpose, however, is to show relationships, not delineation of power of authority. The source of the unit is at the bottom of the chart, rather than the top. One type of tree chart is the decision tree. (5)

Type-based graphics — Graphics in which text, or type, is the major graphic element. At times, text may be the only element in a graphic. Lists, refers, pull quotes and summaries are all text-based graphics. (6)

Typesize — The vertical length of type, measured in points from the highest descender of a letter of type to the lowest ascender. (6)

Word charts — These charts use relatively few words to indicate a much larger set of information. Symbols, pictures, drawings and other graphics are not imperative to understanding the information being presented. These charts generally follow the concept of an outline. The most effective word charts have a unifying theme and try to make a specific point, rather than simply presenting a batch of information about a topic. (5)

x-height — The size (in points) of most lowercase letters of a particular type. (Those letters that extend from the baseline to the top of a lowercase x.) X-height can vary greatly from typeface to typeface, and its relationship to other parts of the typeface is important. In many typefaces, the larger the x-height, the more readable the type will be at smaller point sizes. (6)

Index

Accuracy, 36, 137-140, 162, 165
    adherence to, 26
Adobe Illustrator, 133
Aldus FreeHand, 133
Attriubtion, 37, 38, 165
Axis, 38, 165

Balance, 21-22, 165
Bar chart, 41-46, 58, 155, 166 (see also column charts)
    development by Playfair, 11
    grouped, 43-44, 167
    pictographs, 46, 169
    range, 170
    simple, 41-43, 171
    subdivided, 44-46, 171
Matthew Brady, 130

Calvin and Hobbes, 32
Canaanite alphabet, 94

Caricature, 121
Conrad Wise Chapman, 125
Charleston Daily Mail, 129
Chart-based graphics, 35-59, 166
    categories in, 166
    consistency, 37, 166
    elements, 37-41
    functions, 56
    simplicity, 36-37
Chicago Tribune, 1-2, 3, 4
    Palatine massacre, 1-2
Clip art, 131-132
Color, 37
Column charts, 47-49, 58, 166
    grouped, 48
    range or floating bar, 48-49
    simple, 47-48, 171
    stacked, 48
    time intervals in, 48, 149
Computer-generated illustration, 120, 123

Copyright law, 131, 132-135
Cosmograph, 81-82, 90, 166
Franklin Crawford, 76

Scott Davis, 30, 49, 76, 134, 160
Deadlines, 7
René Decartes, 10, 17
Depth, 28, 29, 39-41, 167
Design
    balance, 21-22
    focus and contrast, 20-21, 166, 167
    principles, 20-26, 31
    unity, 22-23
Brad Diller, 30, 129, 134
Drop cap, 106, 108

Earthquakes, 6
    measurement of, 143-144, 145
Eastman Kodak timeline, 89
Egyptians
    development of calendar, 9
Errors and inaccuracy, 137-152
    avoiding, 151-152
    common practices, 145-150
    sources of error, 140-145

Fact boxes, 112-114
Fair use, copyright law, 131, 133-135, 167
Flow charts, 80-81, 90, 167
Focus and contrast, 20-21
Edwin Forbes, 125

Elbridge Gerry and the gerrymander map, 77
Gettysburg address, 101, 107
Graphic journalists, 14
Graphics
    categorizing, 33
    charts, 35-59
    clarity in, 166
    conventions of, 26-31
    depth, 31
    development of, 154-55
    disadvantages of, 14-15, 17
    errors in, 137-152
    hardware and software for, 155, 161
    in small publications, 156, 157
    principles of presentation, 19-33
    proportionality in, 27-31
    purpose and content, 24-26
    readers, 15-16
    revolution, 4-8, 17
    style and stylebook, 159
    tips from the pros, 30
    type-based, 95-115
    unity in, 22-23
    uses of, 8
Greeks and the alphabet, 94-95
Johann Gutenberg, 95
Gutenberg Bible, 95

Harper's magazine, 124, 125
Ernest Hart, 7, 13, 30, 69
Tracy Hermann, 1
Headlines, 37, 38, 162, 167-168
Nigel Holmes, 61
Winslow Homer, 124

Icons, 137, 133, 168
Illustration-based graphics, 117-136, 155,
    168
    caricature, 121
    clip art, 131-132
    computer generated illustration, 120, 123
    copyright, 131
    creating, 127-131
    icons, 128. 133
    legal and ethical considerations, 132-135
    logos, 127, 133
    permission for use, 132-133
    purposes, 120-122, 133
Inflation, 148

Jackson (Miss.) Clarion-Ledger, 2-3, 4, 7, 8,
    63, 69
    accident on "The Stack," 2-3
    murder of Medgar Evers, 13
David Jahntz, 2
Godfrey Jones, 3

Icons, 128

Kerning, 99, 102, 114, 168
Knoxville News-Sentinel, 7

Labels on charts, 38, 168
Leading, 98, 100-101, 114, 168
Legend, 38, 39, 168-169
Leonardo da Vinci, 9-10, 17
Abraham Lincoln, Gettysburg address, 101, 107
Line chart, 50-54, 58, 169
    area or surface, 52-53
    band or silhouette, 54
    development by Playfair. 11
    multiple, 52
    simple, 50-51
    spikes, 171
Lists, 106, 108
Logos, 127. 133

MacDraw, 133
Maps, 9, 12-14, 61-78
    contour, 66, 68
    data, 68-75, 76, 167
    dot, 73, 167
    explanatory, 75-77
    files, 69
    history, 63-65
    isoline, 73-74, 168
    locator, 65-68, 76, 169
    mislocation in, 150, 151
    proportions in, 149
    relief, 66, 68
    shaded, 70-73
Mercator, 62, 64-65, 76
Charles Joseph Minard, 12

Nashville Banner, 129
Thomas Nast, 124
New York Times, 61, 64
Newspaper technology
    time line, 88-89
19th century illustrators, 124-125, 133
Numbers
    use in graphics, 6-8

Jacqueline Kennedy Onassis, 88
Organization charts, 82-84, 169

Steve Pasternack, 4
Periodical table of elements, 86

Perspective, 29, 31, 39-41, 169
Phoencians and the alphabet, 94-95
Picas
    as measurement of type, 100
Pictorial chart, 85-87, 169
Pie chart, 56-59, 169-170
    conventions of, 56-58
    development by Playfair, 11-12
    elements of, 56
    exploded, 58
Plato, 19
William Playfair, 10-12, 17
Points, size of type, 97
Gordon Preece, 128
Presidential election, 1992, 24-25
Process charts, 80-82, 90, 170
    cosmograph, 81-82
    flow charts, 80-81
    procedure or progress chart, 81, 90, 170
Dan Procter, 7, 30, 55
Projection, 29
Proportionality, 26-31, 149, 149, 170
Ptolemy, 63-64, 76
    map, 9
Public doman for illustrations, 135
Pull quotes, 110-111, 170

Reading
    left to right, 20, 102
    order, 21
Refers, 109-110, 170
Reverse type, 103, 105
Franklin Roosevelt, 83

Serif and sans serif type, 96, 100, 170-171
    ease of reading, 101
    use of, 102-104
Scales for data, 143, 146, 149-150
Screened type, 103, 104
Scribner's magazine, 125
Simplicity, 36-37, 156, 171
Singapore
    graphic of caning, 15
Society of Newspaper Design, 140
Dr. John Snow, 68-70
    map of London, 70
Laura Stanton, 1

Structural charts, 80, 90
  pictorial charts, 85-87, 90
  organization charts, 82-84, 90
  tree charts, 84-85, 90
  word charts, 86, 87, 90
Stacy Sweat, 1, 2
Stock indexes, 142-143
Sumerians, 94
Summary boxes, 112-114
Survey research data, 144

Tables, 106-109
Tennessee Valley Authority, 89
Time charts, 80, 87-90, 155, 171
Time interval in charts, 149, 150
Time magazine, 61
Tree charts, 84-85, 171
Edward Tufte, 32, 35
Type
  all caps, 104
  anatomy of, 96-97, 98-100
  boldface, 103, 104-105, 166
  development of, 94-98
  families of, 99-100
  fonts, 97
  guidelines for use, 114
  italics, 103, 104, 168
  kerning, 99, 102, 114, 168
  leading, 98, 100-101, 114
  measurement of, 97, 100
  reverse, 103, 105
  scaling, 105, 106
  screened, 103, 105
  serif and sans serif, 96, 100,
  101, 102-104, 170-171
  size of, 97, 100, 172
  styles of, 96, 102
  x-height of, 97, 100
Type-based graphics, 93-115, 171-
  172
  drop cap, 106
  lists and tables, 106-109
  pull quotes, 110-111, 170
  refers, 109-110, 170
  summary and fact boxes, 112-
  114

Unity, 22
USA Today, 14
  use of refers, 109
Sandra Utt, 4

Vanishing point, 29
Frank Vizetelly, 125

Watergate, 114
Waud, A.R. 124
Waud, William, 124
White space, 23, 157-158
Winnipeg Free Press, 128
Word charts, 86-87, 172
World Cup soccer tournament,
  138-139

x-axis, 38
x-height of type, 96, 100, 172

y-axis. 38